The Crafter's Design Library

Men's Motifs

Sharon Bennett

David and Charles
www.mycraftivity.com

... and this is for Clayton John and Bradley James

A DAVID & CHARLES BOOK
Copyright © David & Charles Limited 2009

David & Charles is an F+W Media, Inc. company
4700 East Galbraith Road
Cincinnati, OH 45236

First published in the UK in 2009

Illustrations copyright © Sharon Bennett 2009

ISBN-13: 978-0-7153-3045-6 hardback
ISBN-10: 0-7153-3045-4 hardback

ISBN-13: 978-0-7153-3288-7 paperback
ISBN-10: 0-7153-3288-0 paperback

Printed in China by Donnelley Shenzhen
for David & Charles
Brunel House   Newton Abbot   Devon

Commissioning Editor: Jane Trollope
Desk Editor: Emily Rae
Project Editor: Ame Verso
Art Editor: Sarah Clark
Designer: Sabine Eulau and Eleanor Stafford
Production Controller: Ros Napper
Photographer: Karl Adamson

Visit our website at www.davidandcharles.co.uk

David & Charles books are available from all good bookshops; alternatively you can contact our Orderline on 0870 9908222 or write to us at FREEPOST EX2 110, D&C Direct, Newton Abbot, TQ12 4ZZ (no stamp required UK only); US customers call 800-289-0963 and Canadian customers call 800-840-5220

Contents

The essential techniques

The templates

Magical
makes for men

If you've ever found yourself wracking your brains, desperately trying to think of a suitable present for a man – whether for your father, brother, colleague or friend – then this is the book for you! Why men are so hard to buy for is one of life's eternal mysteries, but all that anguish can be avoided by abandoning shop-bought items in favour of more personal, handcrafted cards and gifts.

The Crafter's Design Library: Men's Motifs is a collection of over 400 images that can be used to create your own unique craft projects, perfect for men and boys. From simple greetings cards to customized clothing, key rings, coasters, trinket boxes and even mugs and glasses, this book will give you hundreds of ideas, so you will never again be short of an appropriate gift for the men in your life.

Because there are so many designs to choose from, the book has been divided into seven

easy-to-use chapters to help you find what you are looking for. Whether it's a design to depict his favourite sport, or one to show his job, hobby, or cause for celebration, there are designs for everything and everyone included.

All of the motifs are depicted as simple black-and-white outline drawings, which are easy to photocopy or scan into your computer and then use in whatever way you want. The designs can be simplified, adapted or embellished to suit your needs, and colour choices are left completely up to you.

Whether you are new to crafting or more experienced, be sure to look at the first section of the book, which provides useful information on applying the motifs to different craft media, explains how to adapt and combine designs and gives pointers on key craft techniques. Pages 20–25 feature a fantastic gallery of projects that will help inspire you and give you the confidence you need to start using your selected motifs to create some truly magical makes for men.

Sentiments and sayings

Lost for words? While there are motifs in this book for every situation, sometimes finding the right words can be more of a task. Here are some great ideas that work with key motifs in each chapter to get you started ...

Sport

Hats off to you

You're the best catch

You're my target

Dive straight in

You bowl me over

Right on cue

Transport

Out of this world

Rocket man

Drive me crazy

Just the ticket

The sky's the limit

Long distance lover

Keep on truckin'

Working Life

Champion DIY dad

You know the drill

I've got your measure

Light my fire

Super sleuth

Boys' Toys

If music be the food of love

With all good cheer

You're in control

Virtually yours

It's all in the game

Roll out the barrel

We're on the same

wavelength

Occasions

Disco dad

You're a real winner

Let's shake on it

Take it easy

Suited and booted

Hobbies

You mean the world

to me

Pick of the crop

Hello sunshine

Chip of the old block

Play your cards right

Hot stuff

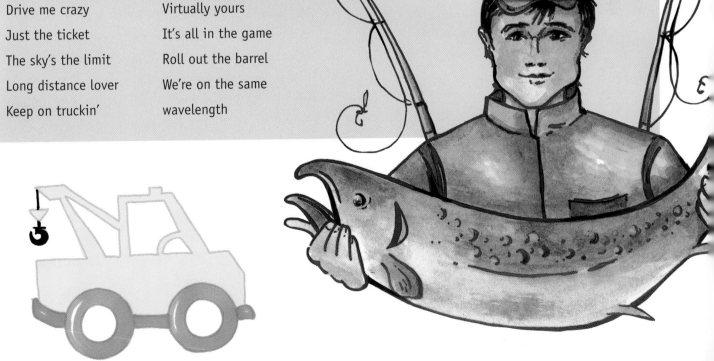

Applying motifs to craft media

The techniques best suited to applying your selected motif to a particular medium depend on the surface you are working with. The following pages offer some simple advice on how to do this for the most popular craft media. Guidance is also given on how to enlarge or reduce the motif to suit your requirements (below) and how to create a stencil (page 11).

Enlarging and reducing a motif

Here are three ways to change the size of a motif to suit your project: the traditional method using a grid, or the modern alternatives of a photocopier or scanner.

Using a grid

The traditional method of enlargement involves using a grid. To begin, use low-tack masking tape to secure tracing paper over the original design. Draw a square or rectangle onto the tracing paper, enclosing the image (see below). Use a ruler to divide up the square or rectangle into rows of equally spaced vertical and horizontal lines. Complex designs should have lines about 1cm (³⁄₈in) apart; simpler ones can have lines 4cm (1½in) apart.

Now draw a square or rectangle to match your required design size, and draw a grid to correspond with the one you have just drawn over the image, as shown below. You can now begin to re-create the original image by redrawing it, square by square, at the required scale.

Using a photocopier

For fast and accurate results, use a photocopier to enlarge or reduce a motif. To do this, you need to calculate your enlargement percentage. First measure the width of the image you want to end up with. Here, the motif needs to be enlarged to 120mm (4¾in). Measure the width of the original motif, which in this case is 60mm (3³⁄₈in). Divide the first measurement by the second to find the percentage by which you need to enlarge the motif, in this instance 200 per cent. (An enlargement must always be more than 100 per cent and a reduction less than 100 per cent).

To photocopy an image onto tracing paper, use tracing paper that is at least 90gsm. When photocopying an image from tracing paper, place the tracing paper onto the glass, and then lay a sheet of white paper on top of it. This will help to produce a sharp copy.

Transferring a motif onto paper, card, wood or fine fabric

A light box makes it easy to trace an image directly onto a piece of paper, thin card or fabric, but if you don't have one it is easy to improvise with household items. Balance a piece of clear plastic across two piles of books or pieces of furniture, and place a table lamp underneath. Place your motif on the plastic and your paper, thin card or fabric on top. Switch on the light and simply trace over the design showing through.

To transfer a design onto wood, thick card or foam, trace the design onto tracing paper using a sharp pencil. Turn the tracing over and redraw on the wrong side with a soft lead pencil. Now turn the tracing over again and use masking tape to secure it right side up onto your chosen surface. Carefully redraw the image (see the photograph below). Press firmly enough to transfer the motif, but take care not to damage the surface.

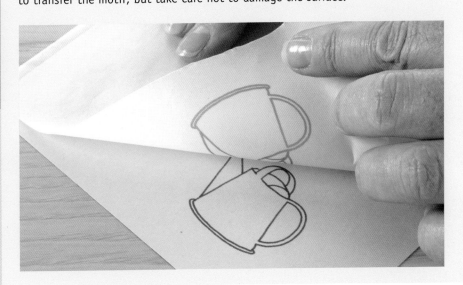

Using a scanner

A third way to enlarge or reduce a motif is to scan the original image on a flatbed scanner or to photograph it with a digital camera. Once the image is on your computer you can either adjust the size using image-manipulation software or simply alter the percentage of your printout size. If the finished result is larger than the printer's capacity, some software will allow you to tile the image over several sheets of paper, which can then be joined together to form the whole image.

An image-manipulation package may also allow you to alter the proportions of a motif, making it wider or narrower, for example. Take care not to distort it beyond recognition, though. Once you are happy with your image, it can be saved to be used again and again.

Transferring a motif onto foil

To emboss foil, simply take the original tracing and secure it to the foil surface. Rest the foil on kitchen paper. Use an embossing tool or an old ballpoint pen that has run out of ink to press down on the tracing, embossing the metal below. Use the same technique on the back of the foil to produce a raised effect.

Transferring a motif onto mirror and ceramic

Trace the motif onto tracing paper, then turn the tracing over and redraw it on the wrong side using a chinagraph pencil. A chinagraph produces a waxy line that adheres well to shiny surfaces such as coloured glass, mirrored glass and ceramic. Chinagraphs are prone to blunt quickly, but it doesn't matter if the lines are thick and heavy at this stage. Use masking tape to secure the tracing right side up onto the surface. Carefully redraw with a sharp pencil to transfer the image.

Tracing a motif onto glass and acetate

Roughly cut out the motif and tape it to the underside of the acetate or glass with masking tape. It is helpful to rest glassware on a few sheets of kitchen towel for protection and to stop curved objects from rolling. The image will now show through the clear surface, and you can simply trace along the lines with glass outliner or paint directly onto the surface.

If you want to transfer an image onto opaque glass, or onto a container that is difficult to slip a motif behind, such as a bottle with a narrow neck, follow the instructions on page 7 for transferring a motif onto mirror and ceramic.

Transferring a motif onto curved items

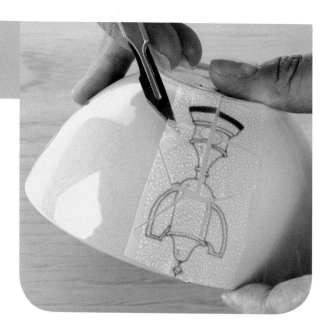

Motifs can be transferred onto rounded items, but will need to be adapted to fit the curves. First trace the motif, redrawing it on the underside (use a chinagraph pencil if the container is ceramic). Make cuts in the template from the edge towards the centre. Lay the motif against the surface so that the cuts slightly overlap or spread open, depending on which way the surface curves. Tape the motif in place with masking tape and transfer the design by drawing over the lines with a sharp pencil.

Making a template for a straight-sided container

If you wish to apply a continuous motif such as a border to a straight-sided container, make a template of the container first. To do this, slip a piece of tracing paper into a transparent glass container or around an opaque glass or ceramic container. Lay the paper smoothly against the surface and tape in place with masking tape. Mark the position of the upper edge of the container with a pencil. Now mark the position of the overlapping ends of the paper or mark each side of the handle on a mug, cup or jug.

Remove the tracing and join the overlap marks, if you have made these. Measure down from the upper edge and mark the upper limit of the band or border on the template. Cut out the template and slip it into or around the container again to check the fit. Transfer your chosen template onto the tracing paper, then onto the container.

Making a template for a plate

1 Cut a square of tracing paper slightly larger than the diameter of the plate. Make a straight cut from one edge to the centre of the paper then roughly cut out a circle from the centre to help the paper lie flat. Place the paper centrally on the plate or saucer and tape one cut edge across the rim. Smooth the paper around the rim and tape in place, overlapping the cut edges. Mark the position of the overlap on the paper.

2 Turn the plate over and draw around the circumference onto the underside of the tracing paper. Remove the paper, then measure the depth of the plate rim and mark it on the paper by measuring in from the circumference. Join the marks with a curved line.

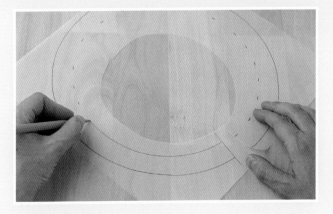

Transferring a motif onto fabric

If fabric is lightweight and pale in colour, it may be possible to trace the motif simply by laying the fabric on top. If the fabric is dark or thick, it may help to use a light box. Place the motif under the fabric on the surface of the light box (see page 7 for information on constructing a home light box). As the light shines up through the motif and fabric you should be able to see the design lines, ready for tracing.

Alternatively, place a piece of dressmaker's carbon paper face down on the fabric and tape the motif on top with masking tape. Trace the design with a sharp pencil to transfer it onto the fabric, as shown below. The marks made by the carbon are easily wiped away.

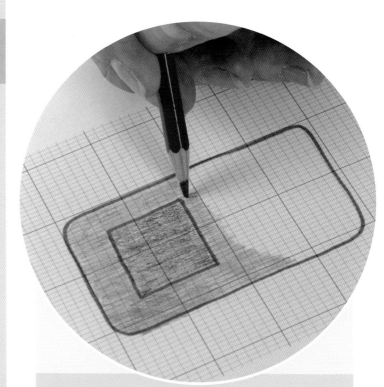

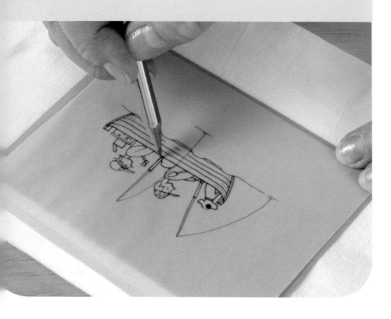

Transferring a motif onto a knitting chart

Always use knitting-chart paper rather than ordinary graph paper to chart a knitting design. Knitted stitches are wider than they are tall and knitting chart paper is sized accordingly. Transfer the motif straight onto the knitting graph paper (see page 7 for advice on transferring a motif onto paper). Each square on the graph paper represents one stitch. Make sure that you are happy with the number of squares in the motif, as this dictates the number of stitches in your design, and ultimately the design size. Fill in the applicable squares on the chart using coloured pens or pencils to denote the yarn colours you are going to use.

Use the finished chart in conjunction with a knitting pattern. Read the chart from right to left for a knit row and from left to right for a purl row. The motif can also be worked with Swiss darning.

Transferring a motif onto needlepoint canvas and cross stitch fabric

Designs on needlepoint canvas and cross stitch fabric can be worked either by referring to the design on a chart, or by transferring the image to the material and stitching over it.

To transfer the motif onto a chart

Transfer the motif straight onto graph paper (see page 7 for advice on transferring onto paper). Each square on the graph paper represents a square of canvas mesh or Aida cross stitch fabric. Colour in the squares that the motif lines cross with coloured pencils or pens. You may want to make half stitches where the motif outline runs through a box. Mark the centre of the design along a vertical and horizontal line (see right) and mark the centre of the fabric lengthways and widthways with tacking stitches.

To transfer the motif directly onto canvas or fabric

With an open-weave canvas or pale fabric it is possible to trace the design directly onto the canvas or fabric. First, mark a small cross centrally on the motif and on the material. On a light box (see page 7 for information on

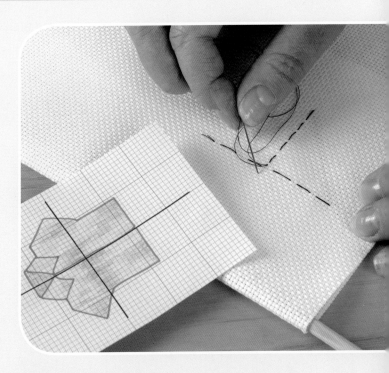

constructing a home light box), place the material on top of the motif, aligning the crosses. Tape in position and trace the image with a waterproof pen. Alternatively, use dressmaker's carbon paper to transfer the design, as explained in transferring a motif onto fabric, opposite.

Making a stencil

Tape a piece of tracing paper over the motif to be adapted into a stencil. Redraw the image, thickening the lines and creating 'bridges' between the sections to be cut out. You may find it helpful to shade in the areas to be cut out. Lay a piece of carbon paper, ink side down, on a stencil sheet, place the tracing on top, right side up, and tape in place. Redraw the design to transfer it to the stencil sheet. Finally, lay the stencil sheet on a cutting mat and carefully cut out the stencil with a craft knife, always drawing the sharp edge of the blade away from you.

Adapting and combining designs

Although you can use the templates in this book exactly as they are, a lot of fun can be had by messing around with them, simplifying designs, reversing or repeating them, combining them and so on. You can do this endlessly, making your library of templates never-ending as your ideas become new images.

Simplify it

Most motifs that have a lot of detail in them can work just as well in a more simplified version. These slippers from page 96 have had the detail taken out and now rely on the outline only – they could now be coloured with a solid tone.

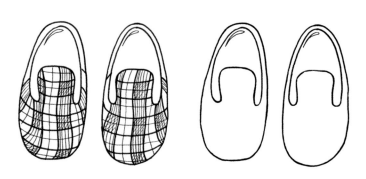

Make a silhouette

Turning a design into a silhouette requires that you take just the outline and fill in the shape. This is most effective when using a black image on a coloured background, but gold on a dark background also looks dramatic. The motif here is the motorbike from page 79.

Flip it

By flipping a motif you can increase its uses, making it possible to combine it with other motifs in different ways. Here, the banner from page 89 has been used in its original form with the beer pump from page 74 and flipped with the darts from page 38.

Sometimes a motif wont fit into the space you have but by flipping it in the other direction it will work.

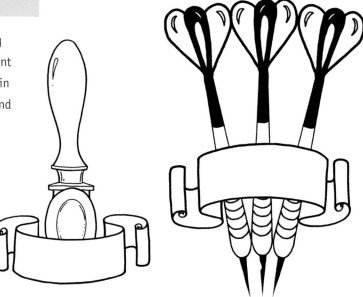

Combine images

You can create your own designs by combining two or more images together. Here, the chair from page 96 has been used in two ways: the first has the reading figure from page 96 added to it, and the second features the fishing boy from page 110. Get into the habit of really looking at motifs and working out how you can mix and match them.

If the two designs that you want to combine are very different in scale, you will have to enlarge or reduce them on a photocopier or scan them into the computer (see pages 6–7).

Make a border

Flip and repeat motifs to create eye-catching borders. The drill from page 61, for example, makes a great decorative border.

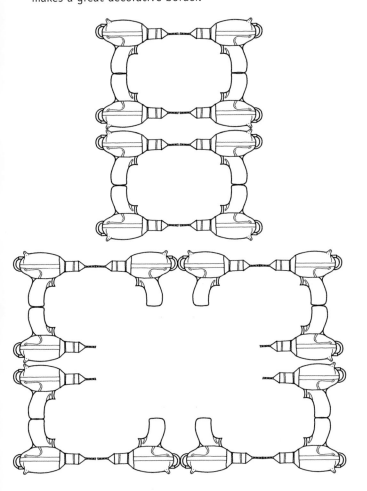

Build it up

You can adapt a motif to suit your own requirements by changing it however you like. Here, the burger from page 105 has been transformed into an enormous American-style burger. Each section has been made by repeating the burger and bottom bun without the base line.

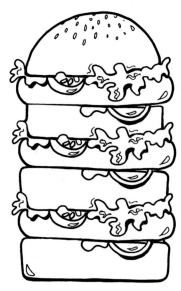

Techniques and media

Trying out different techniques and media is a good way of stretching your creativity, so don't limit yourself to the same materials you've always used – take the opportunity to try something new. Here's just a sample to whet your appetite.

Embossing

These days many of us use a stencil for embossing, but this isn't strictly necessary. Trace your image, turn over the tracing and lay it on foil or vellum. Place both layers on a piece of stiff foam, such as an upturned mouse mat, and go over the lines carefully, without pressing too hard. Now just turn over the foil or vellum and apply it to your card or other item. Here, the cup motif from page 40 was embossed onto gold foil and then glued onto a piece of stamped card.

When you have your embossed image, make sure you look at both sides to check which will work best – the indented side or the raised side; both can be used.

Stencilling

This is an easy and enjoyable way of using a motif. Make your stencil as explained on page 11, making sure you keep the cut-away sections separate so that a piece of your design doesn't just drop out. Use a stencil brush or sponge to dab small amounts of acrylic paint onto the surface to be stencilled, using more than one colour if desired. Try adding further embellishments to enhance the image.

Combining papers

Making a motif from several different papers can be lots of fun. Simply trace and cut out each section of your image from a different paper, as shown here. Now assemble the layers, starting with those at the back and building up to the details; stick the layers in place. Now you can add detailing with outliners, stick-on gems and so on. These motifs can be found on pages 59 and 63.

When sticking down each section, take extra care to ensure the parts are secured in the correct order.

Fabric painting

There are many fabric paints available on the market but most are designed for either silk or cotton. Silk should be stretched in a frame first, and the design lines drawn with gutta. Once this is dry you can flood silk paint into areas enclosed by a gutta line. Acrylic fabric paints can be used like paint on fabric – sponged, applied with a brush or drawn on.

Here, a white pearl fabric outliner was used to trace over the saxophone motif on page 73. This was then slipped behind a piece of painted silk. Once dry it was folded into a tie shape using the motif on page 59 as a reference.

Gutta is great for adding texture – don't just use it to create areas for painting, use it for the details too.

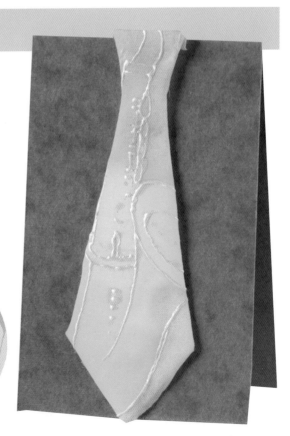

Using a computer

For quick collage, scan images into a computer and print out repeated motifs to cut out and stick down. You can change the colour on the computer or use pens and paints to embellish them later. If desired, you can stick the motifs down with sticky pads to raise them off the surface. The motif used here (see page 105) was drawn with felt pens to achieve a quick, sketchy look and then scanned in and repeated.

Reversing out

This technique is easiest to do on a computer by making the motif white and laying it over an area of colour. Alternatively, you can trace the motif onto coloured paper or card and then paint over the lines with white pen, paint or outliner. Another idea is to trace your design onto white paper, cut it out and stick it onto a coloured base, rather like a white silhouette. The motif used here can be found on page 106.

Tonal images

This shirt motif (see page 59) has been painted in watercolours. Using just one colour in different tones can look stylish and sophisticated, especially when combined with card or embellishments in the same colour. In watercolour you can just dilute the paint to make lighter and lighter colours, but with other media you could add white paint. Adding white gives a creamy effect to the colours and provides flat coverage whereas diluting with water creates translucency.

Using the motif in one colour and placing it onto a paler version of same colour is a simple yet successful tonal effect.

Using outliners

Outliners aren't just for silk fabrics and ceramics – they work fabulously well on paper too. Outliners are often considered just for embellishing your card items, such as this tennis card (see page 31), but they can be really great for producing great stylish cards in their own right, like this baby face card (see page 83). Make sure you leave the outliner to dry for sufficient time before handling the design so that you don't smudge it.

Choosing a medium

Deciding which surface you are going to paint on is the first step in any project. Then you have to look at what paints are suitable and consider the effect you want to achieve. Crafting really does take over so make sure you set aside a clear space to work in and have plenty of time.

Metallic and pearlized paints

Metallic and pearlized paints or paper and board can be used for detail such as trophies and bows but can also be used as backgrounds to give your designs real impact. Try out some of the great holographic papers available; they work particularly well for borders. Metallic paint can be added to give the appearance of chrome on vehicle motifs, for example, or can be used as a highlight to pick up light and give depth. Look out for glitter sealers too, which are clear based and dry to a matte finish but have tiny glitter particles in them that sing out in silver, gold or pearl.

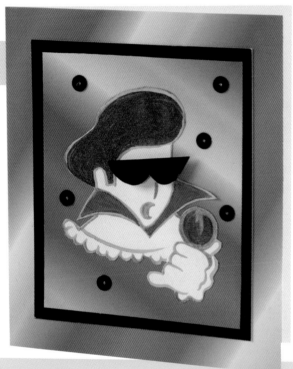

Metal leaf

Usually metal leaf is applied by first painting glue size onto the area to be treated and then applying the metal leaf on top. Another way is to apply the glue as an outliner and then press on special foil. Sometimes you need to apply a hairdryer to complete the process, so check with the manufacturer's instructions. The pipe from page 107 was cut out from thick card and the size was applied all over. Once dry, the gold leaf rubbed on, then gold outliner was used to add the lines.

If you are planning to cut out your motif, as here, you may find it easier to do this before you add the foil detailing – that way you can get the foil right up to the edges.

It was stuck down over the slippers from page 96 with a craft foam pad to give this 3D effect.

Crayons and pencils

This card has been coloured with pencils to match the ceramic items in the Project gallery on page 23, and uses the motif on page 107. The pencil was applied to thick textured card that has a grain, which shows the pencils off to their full advantage. You can always add further detailing and texture to your work with outliner, or look out for water-soluble pencils, which can be washed over with a wet paintbrush to spread the colour.

Pen and ink or watercolours

The fishing boy from page 110 and the Wellington boots from page 44 have been used for very graphic results on the cards here. Outline the design in waterproof pen first and then colour in with inks or watercolours. Bright colours work well with a strong design, while diluted shades give a subtler finish.

Project gallery

Card making is probably the number one use for the templates in this book, but there are times when you will want to treat a friend, yourself or your home to something creative and special. Here are some ideas for using the templates for a variety of items.

Assorted aprons

A single motif can be used to make a diverse range of designs, just by changing the colours and embellishments. Here, three variations have been produced using the apron on page 60. The DIY card was made by adding tool motifs. The barbecue-themed card could be used as an invitation. For the gardening version, a checked background was used with gardening tools and vegetables from pages 108–109.

Most cards can be adapted to make great tags to coordinate with your gift. Use the same papers and scale down the motifs to create the tag.

Get shirty

This card really has the wow factor. The shirt motif from page 59 has been cut from sections of striped paper and stuck over a sheet of tissue paper then layed in a simple box made from black card. Cut-out numerals were secured underneath to create the birthday message. Use small details to finish off the card, such as these shiny buttons, and add a label to the shirt which can be personalized with the name or age of the birthday boy.

When making cards like these cars, you must remember to leave one part uncut along the fold line in order for them to work.

Hot wheels

These funky car cards are sure to get their recipient all revved up. They both use the motif on page 86 but are folded differently. The car motif has been used large as a cut-out shape, and then folded along the side or the top. Number plates are great for adding text, such as a date or a message. Try cutting the car from patterned paper for a really eye-catching effect and making smaller gift tags to complete the ensemble.

Gone fishing

'If the keys are missing, I've gone fishing' is the sentiment behind this sign, which uses the motifs on pages 44 and 110, but it could easily reflect other themes. Try the motifs on pages 108–109 for a gardener, for example. Plain signs are available from craft suppliers ready to be decorated. To make this one, simply paint or découpage the motifs onto a pale green background. A coordinating card will make the gift all the more special.

Raise your glass

Here's a unique gift that any man will love – a personalized glass tankard. The golfer motif from page 100 has been used here, but commemorative dates or motifs associated with special occasions would also work well. Etching motifs onto glass is not as difficult as you might think; all you need are the engraving tools and a steady hand. Battery operated engravers are now stocked in many craft shops and do the job perfectly – simply secure the motif behind the glass while you are working. Alternatively you could use glass paints to create a coloured image.

Bowled over

This ceramic mug, featuring the motif from page 107, would be perfect for a bowls fan. Ceramic paints allow images to be painted on by hand and are then baked in the oven to harden. This makes items durable enough to withstand washing and therefore practical enough to use. A matching gift tag complements the mug.

Any area you don't want painted can be masked off with masking tape. Lay down the colour starting with quite pale, light layers and building it up gradually.

Take a gamble

These plain shop-bought coasters have been decorated with motifs from page 106 to create a fun casino-style set that card players will adore. When working with wood, always make sure you sand off any rough edges with a fine glass paper. Some paints require a primer to be used first, but many acrylics work fine painted straight onto wood, so always read the manufacturer's instructions. Add a layer of clear, quick-drying varnish to make them more durable.

Clever covers

Here's a great gift for guys who can't live without their mobile phone or mp3 player. Create a simple cover from felt fabric, machine stitched on three sides and then turned inside out, then appliqué on the motif of your choice. Alternatively, use the whole cover as the motif, as has been done with the dinner jacket design from page 95. To personalize it even more, you could add his initials and some extra embellishments.

Ship mate

Even men need somewhere to keep their precious treasures. This MDF box was painted white then the lid was divided into four and each part painted. The sides have strips of red paper glued around them, then a collection of nautical images from pages 48–49 stuck on. The life belt emblem allows a photo to be placed behind it. Cards, gift tags and wrapping paper can all be made to coordinate.

Key player

These blank key fobs have been painted with acrylics and have a nice chunky feel to them. The shape of the item you are decorating will dictate the type of motif that is suitable, although you can always use just a part of a design, such as this triangular tag, which features a section of the motif on page 107. Use a matte varnish to protect the design.

Golden goal

Decorating footwear is a great way for kids to recognize their own shoes at school. These pumps have been embellished with the football motif on page 32, which has been painted on with fabric paints and outliners. Why not try glitter fabric pens and puffy fabric pens too, to create one-off customized wearable gifts, with gift tags to match?

Some fabric paints and outliners require heat setting by ironing on the reverse side, which is hard to do on shoes, but is more easily done on bags, t-shirts and hats.

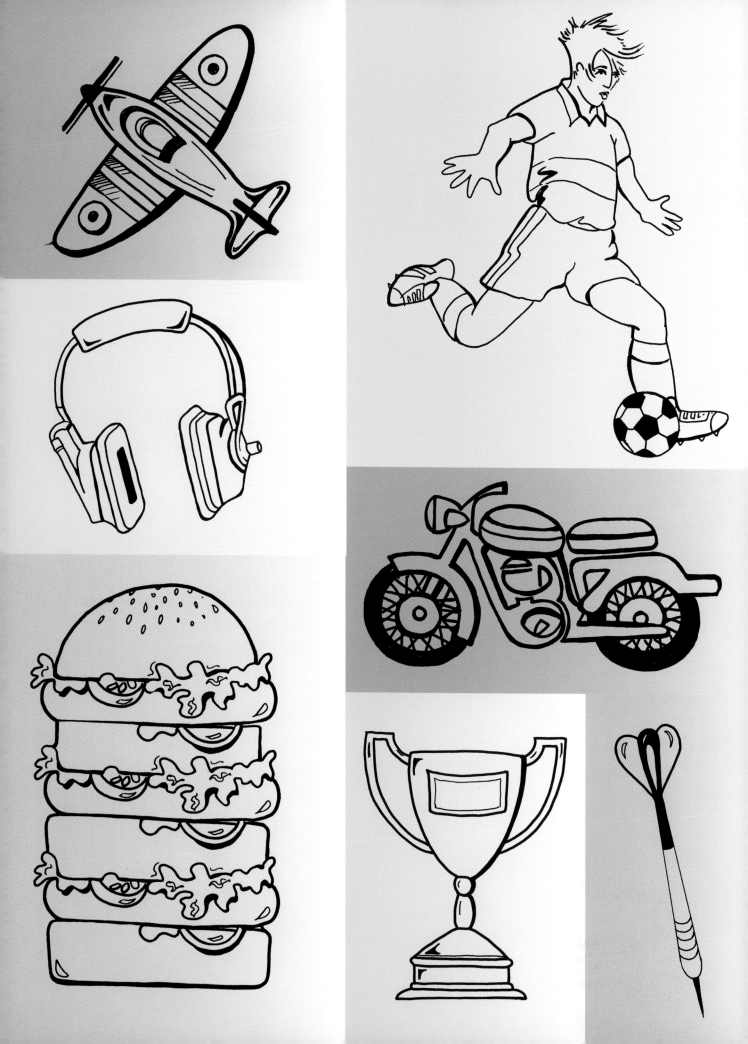

The templates

Sport

If there is one thing all men have in common it is a passion for sport. Whether participating or just spectating, nothing is surer to capture their attention than the spectacle and competition of a sporting event.

This chapter covers all the major sports that the men in your life might be interested in, and kicks off with some of the many types of headgear associated with their favourite activities. Balls of all shapes and sizes follow, and then pages 32–33 give some great motifs for the 'beautiful game' itself – soccer – some of which have been used to create the items shown on page 25.

Whether it is baseball, rugby, cricket, basketball, tennis, hockey, boxing, pub games, martial arts, motor sport, cycling, winter sports or water sports – there are motifs here to encapsulate them all.

Finally, archery, hunting, shooting and fishing emblems complete the collection, giving you all the elements you need to create cards and gifts with an actively energetic theme.

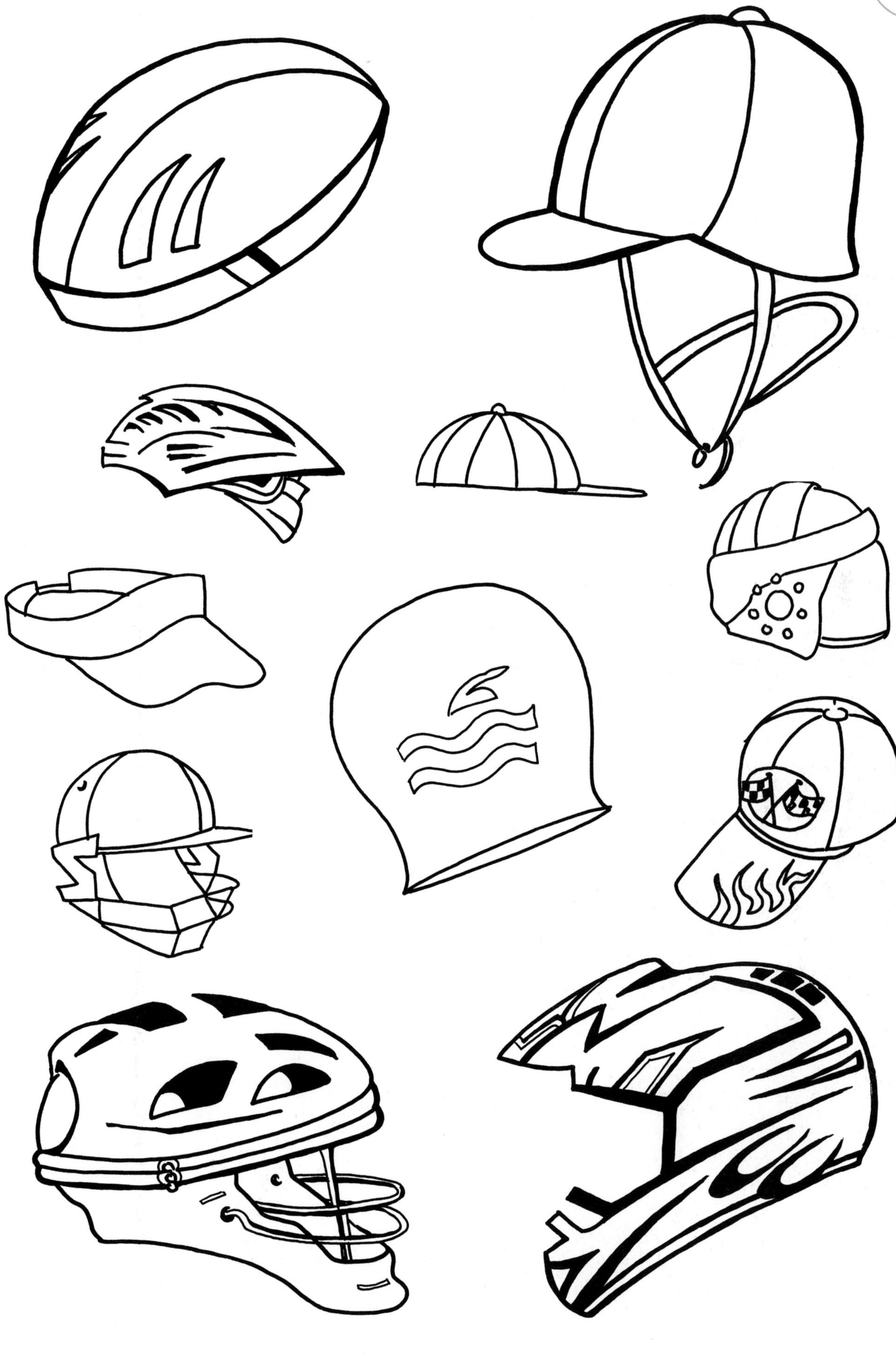

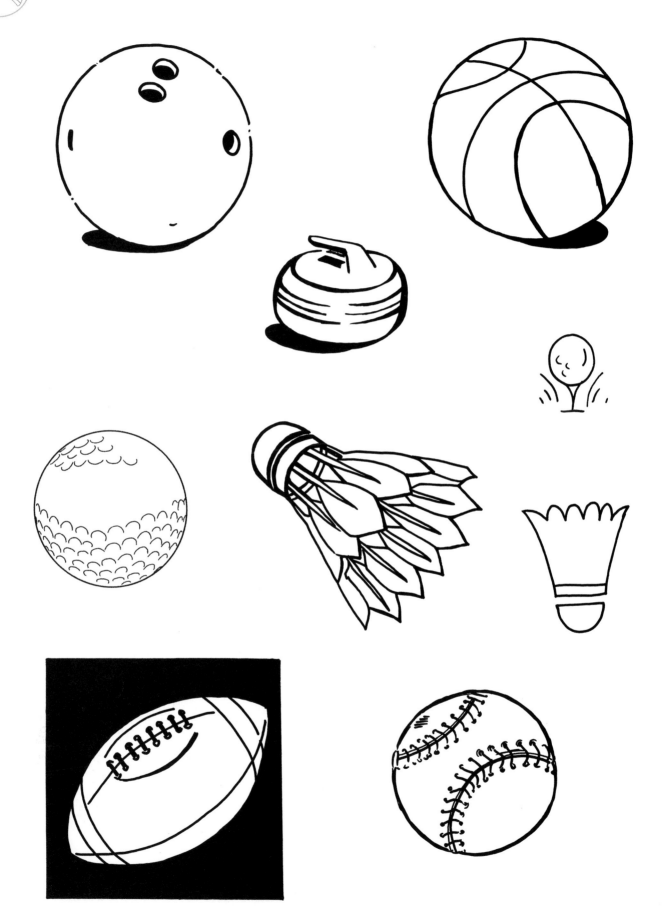

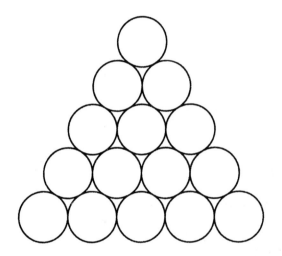

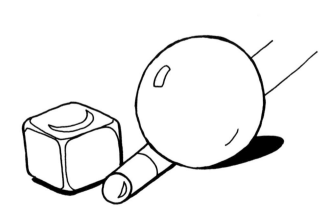

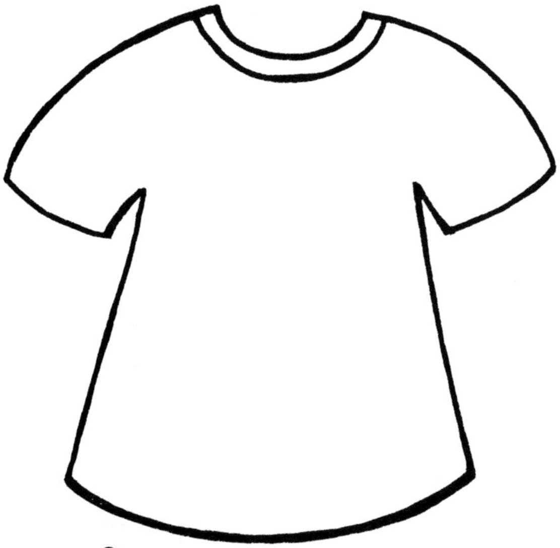

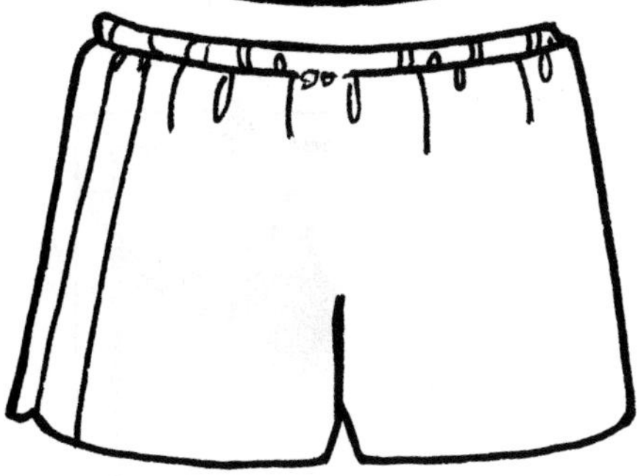

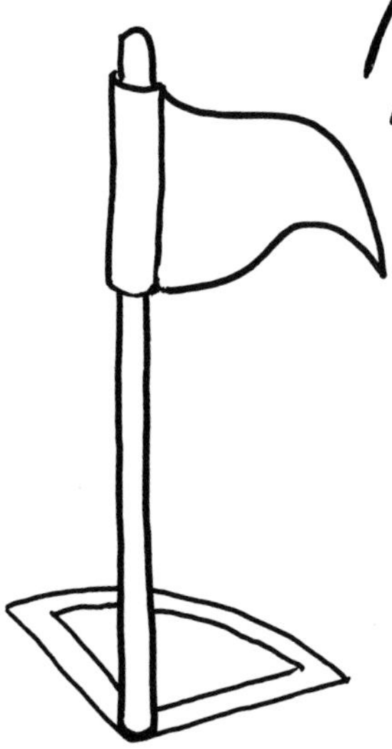

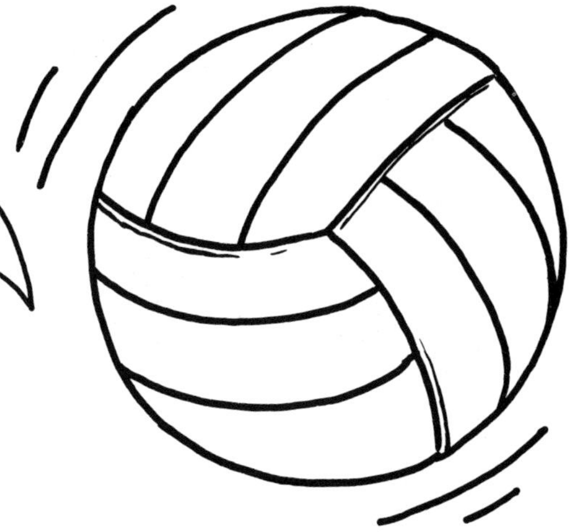

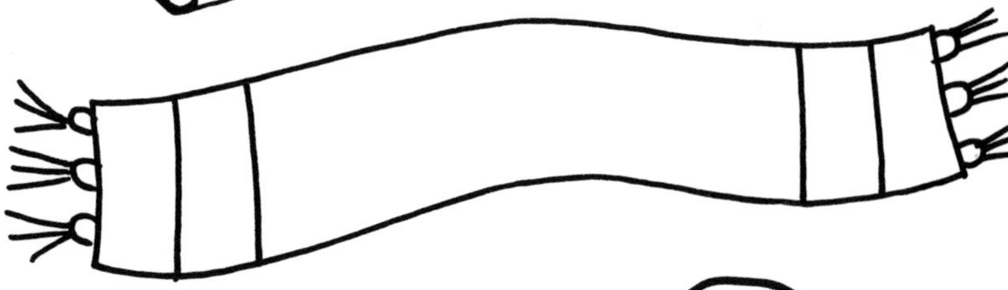

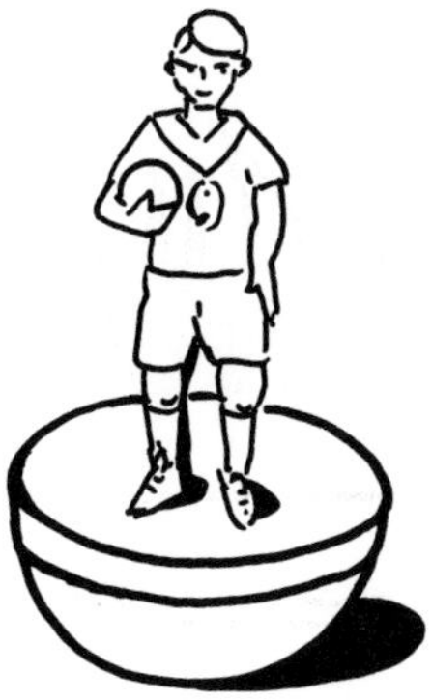

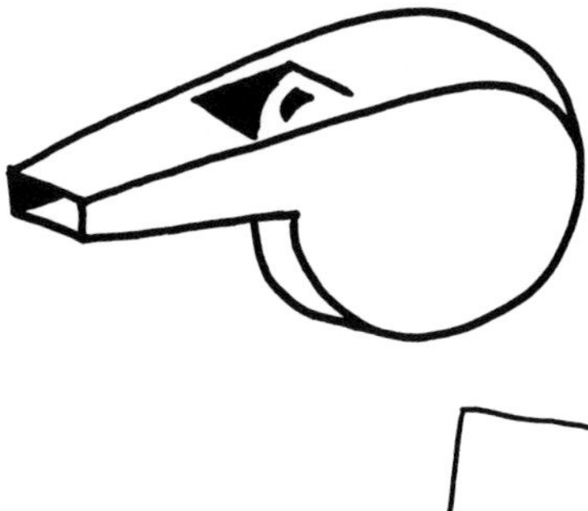

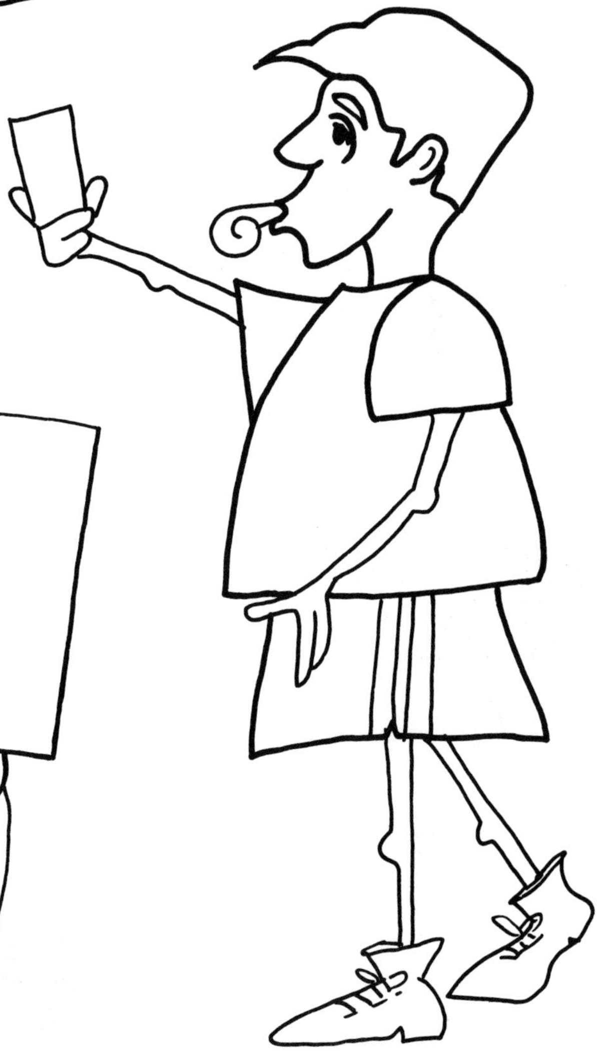

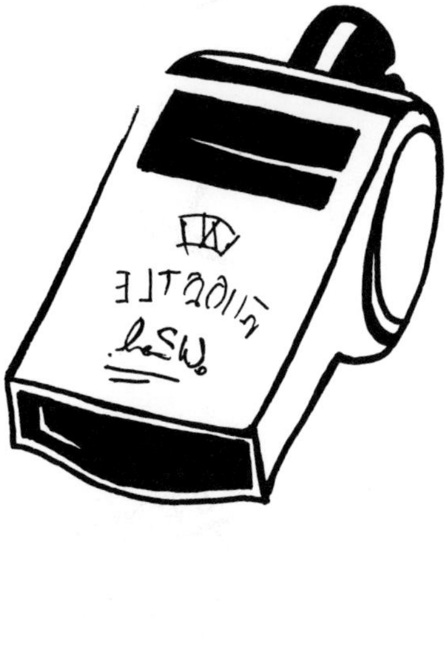

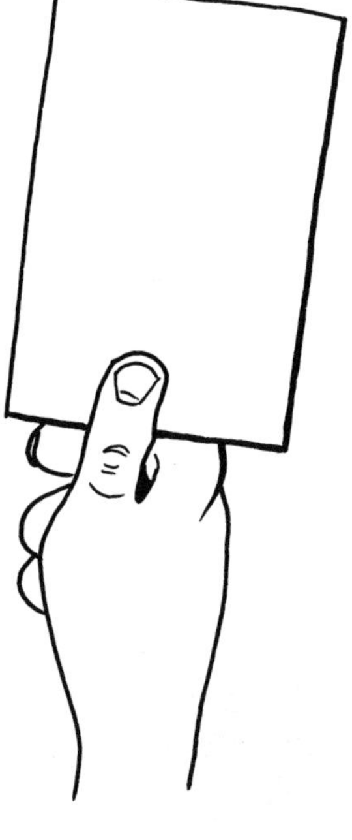

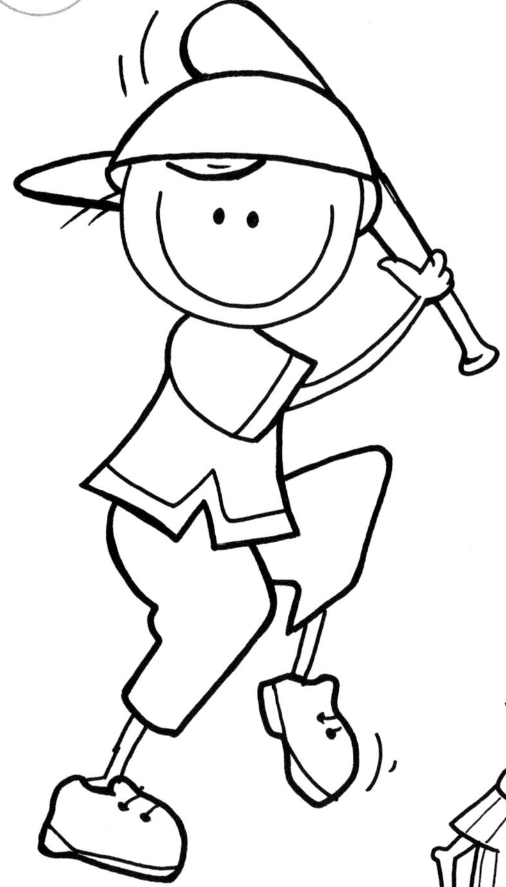

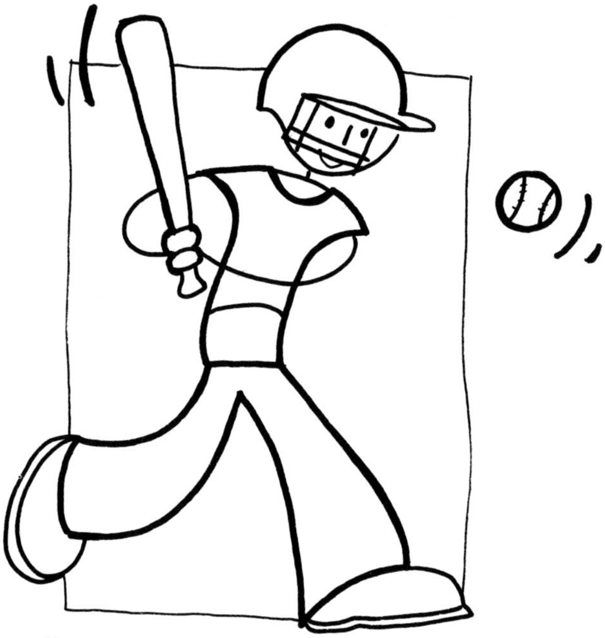

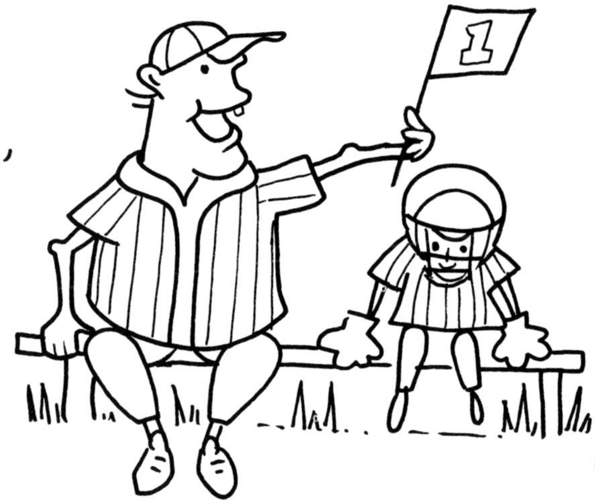
1

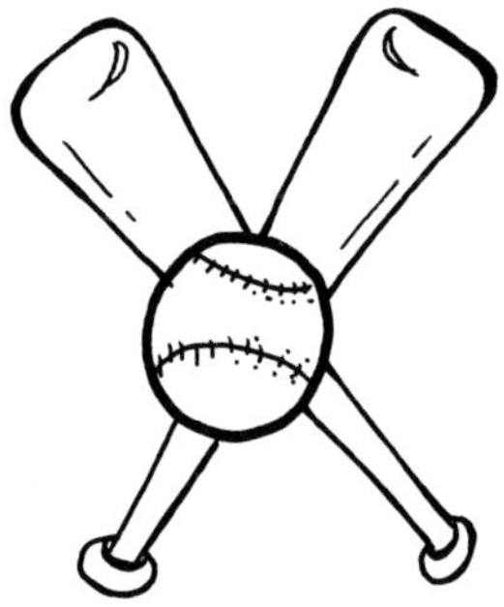

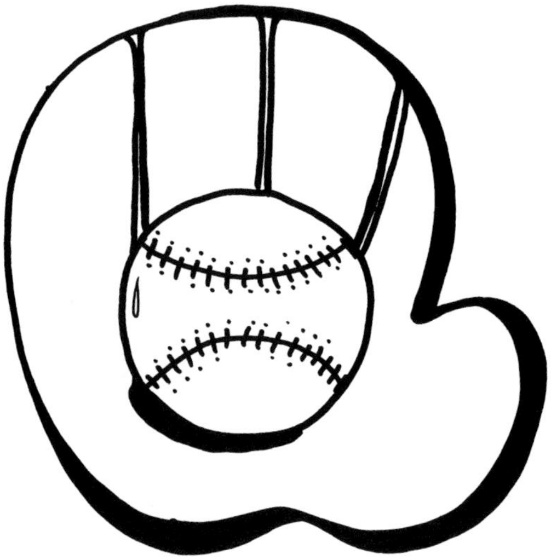

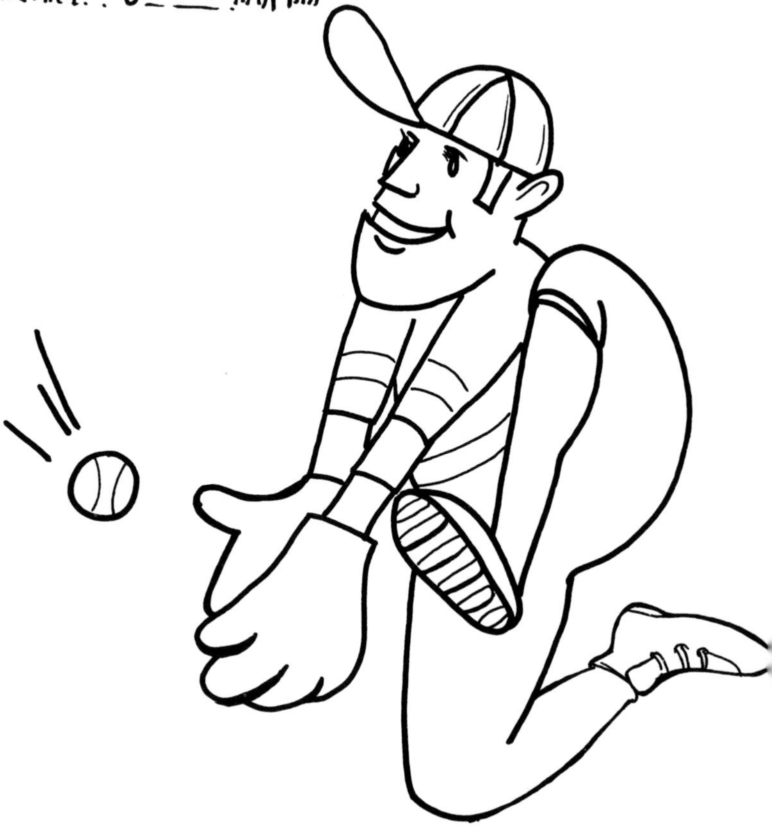

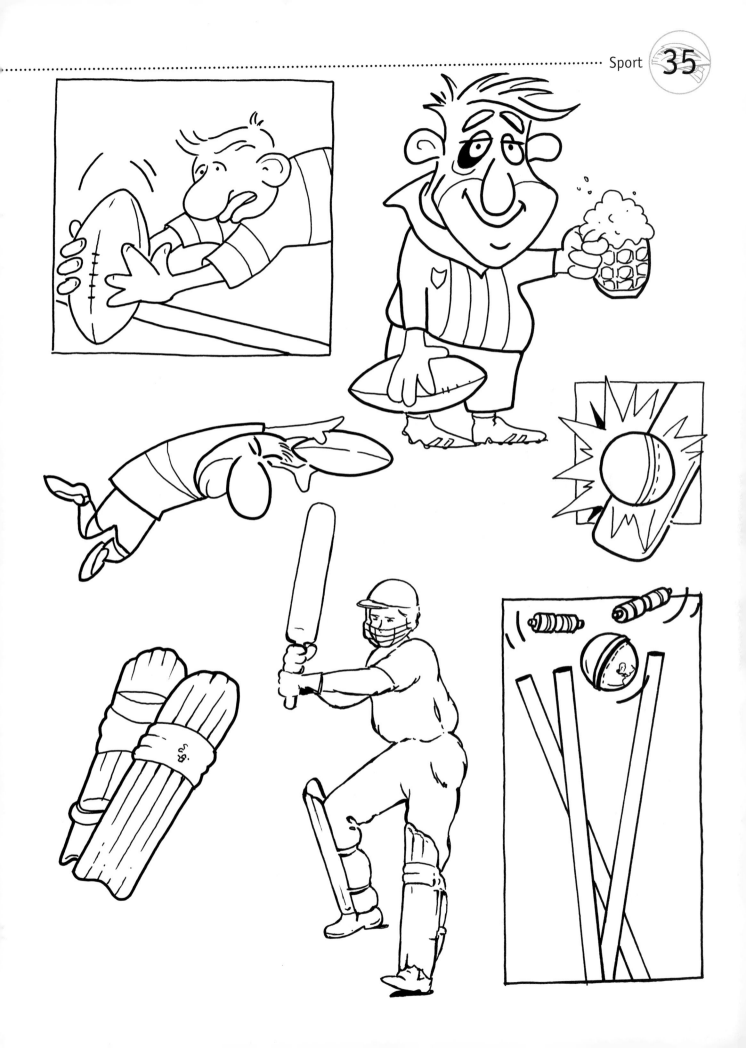

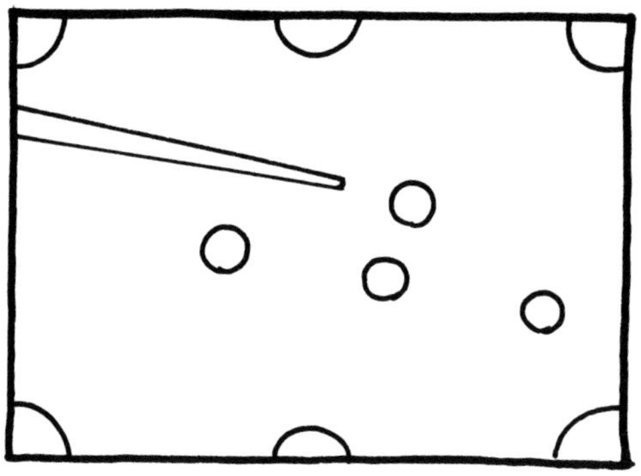

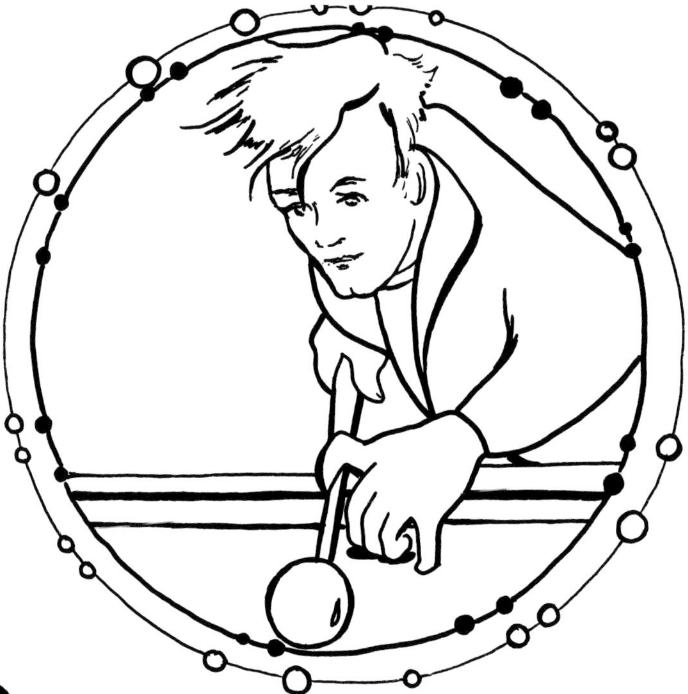

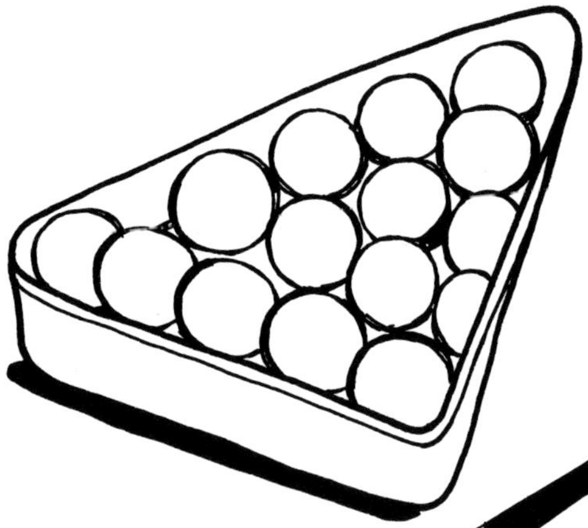

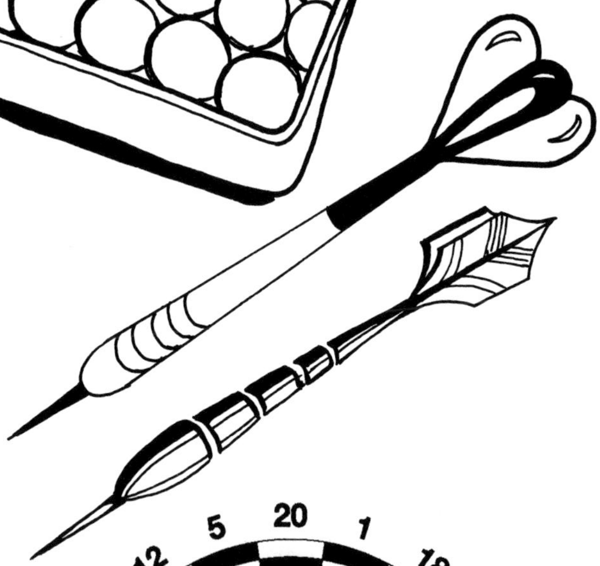

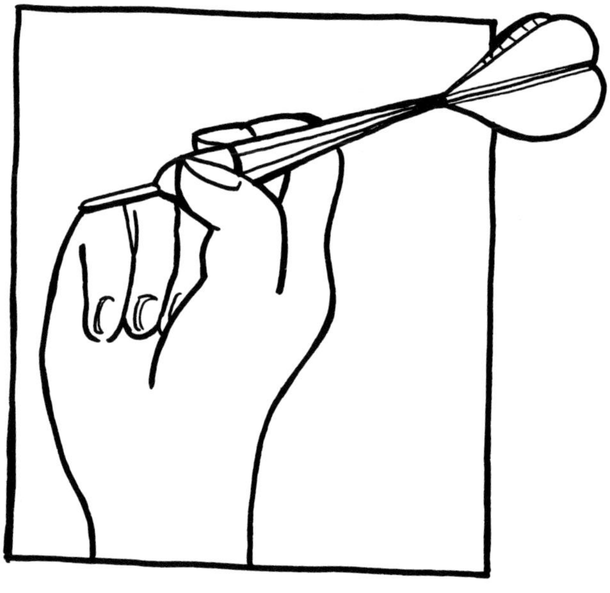

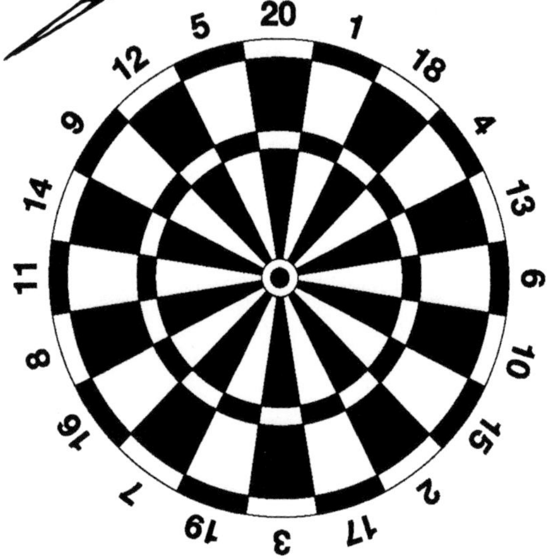
20
1
18
4
13
6
10
15
2
17
3
19
7
16
8
11
14
9
12
5

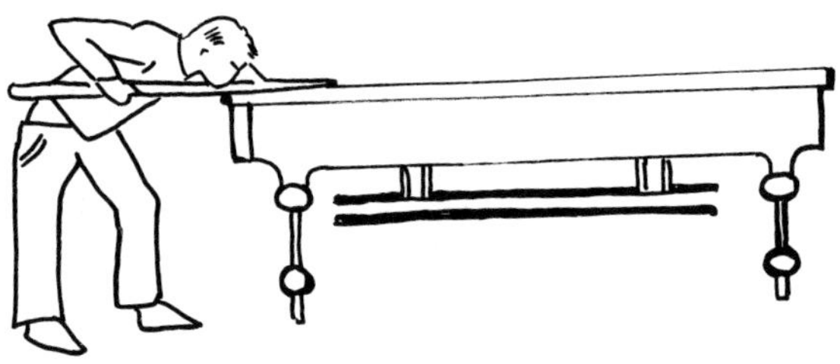

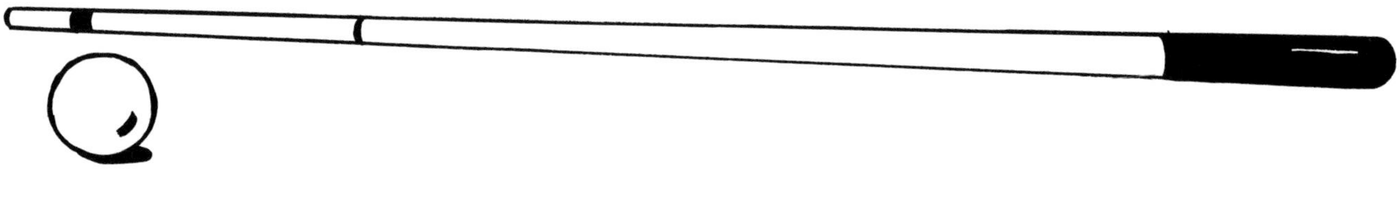

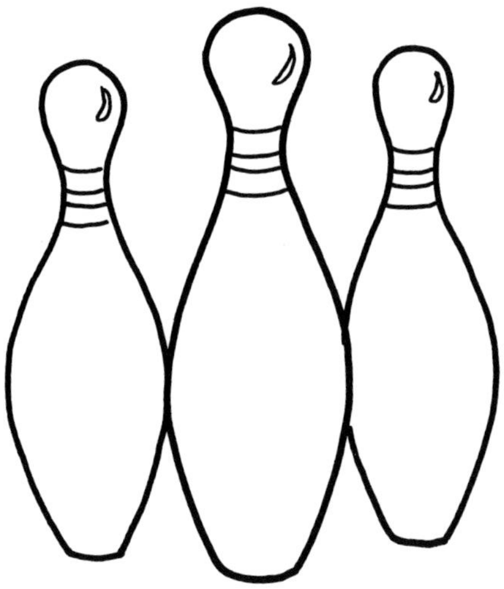

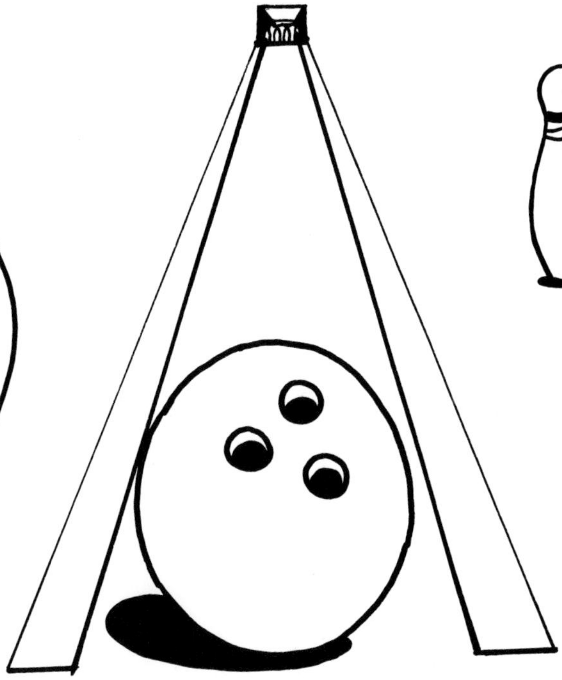

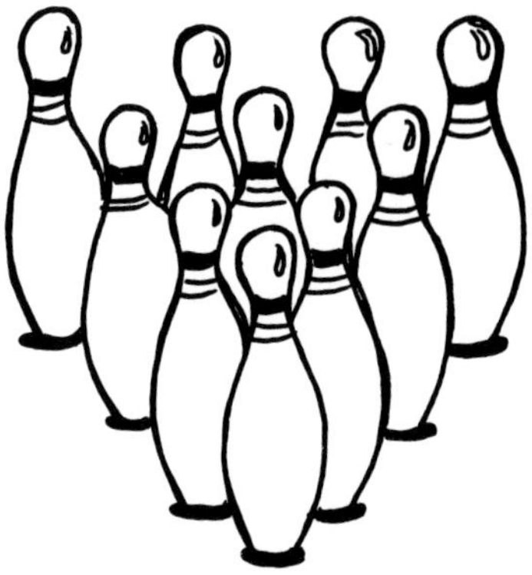

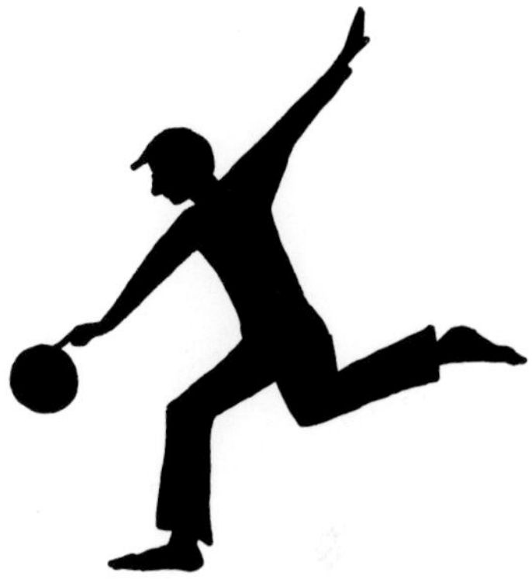

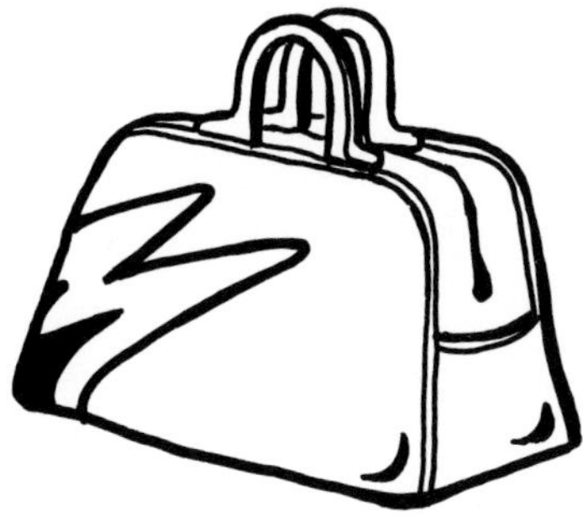

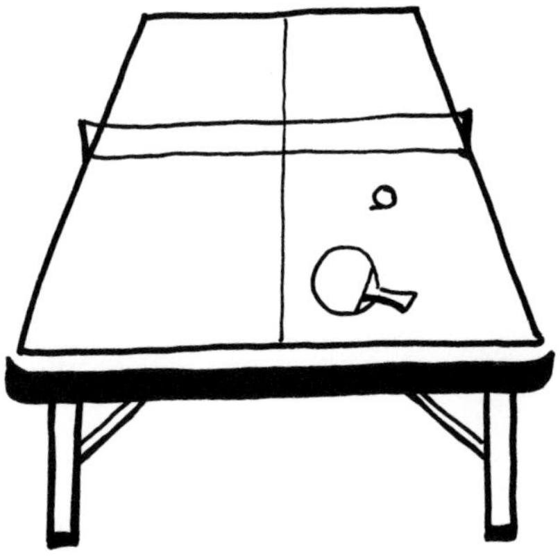

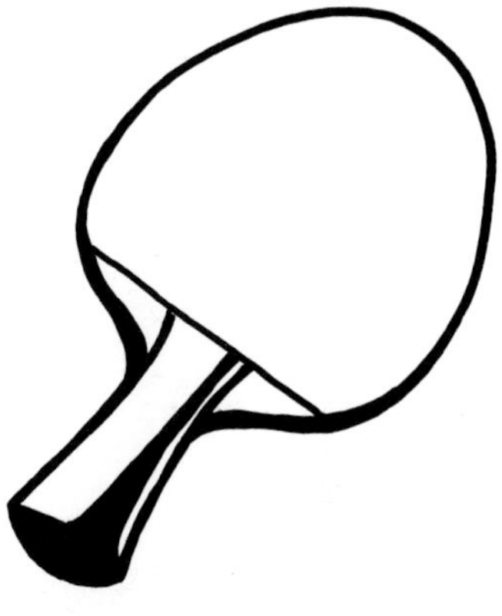

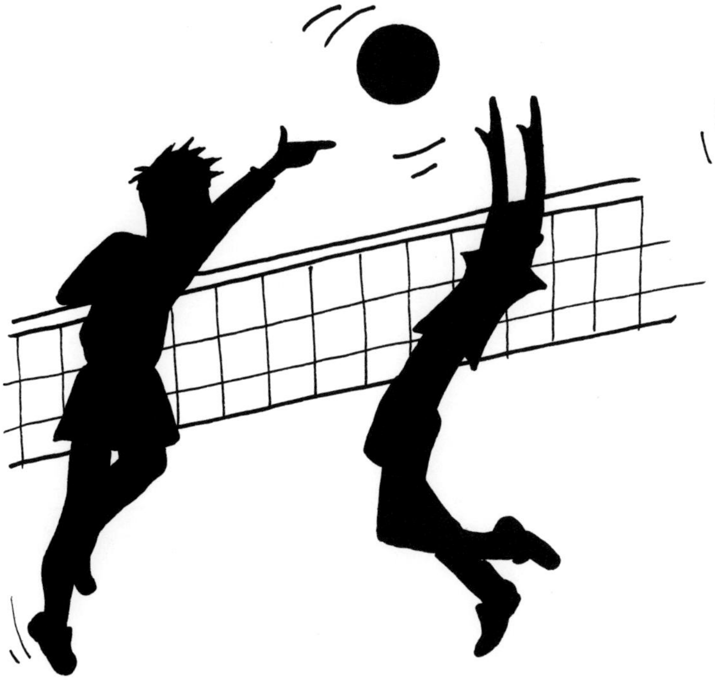

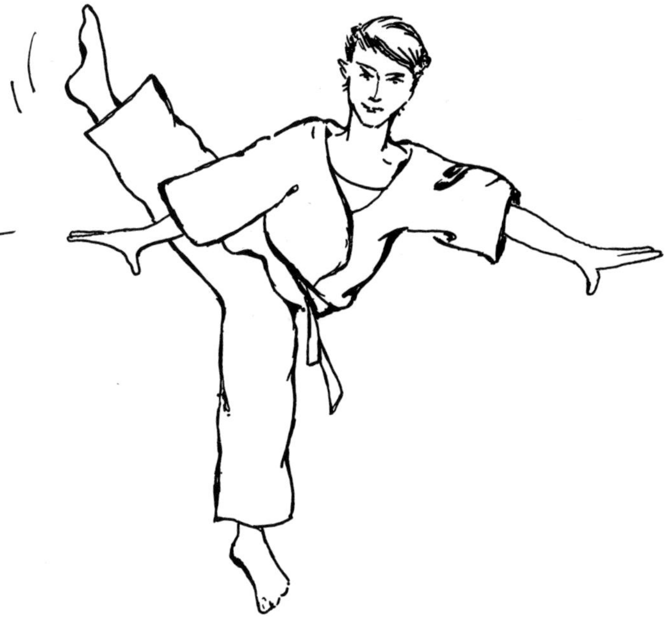

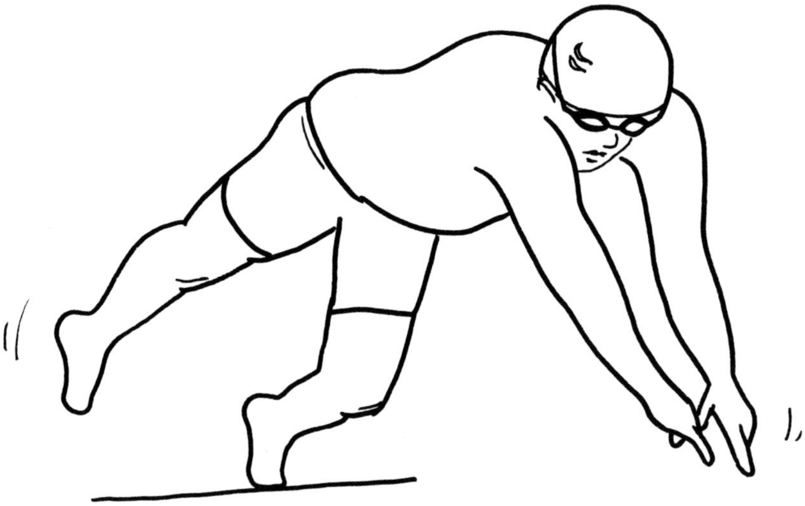

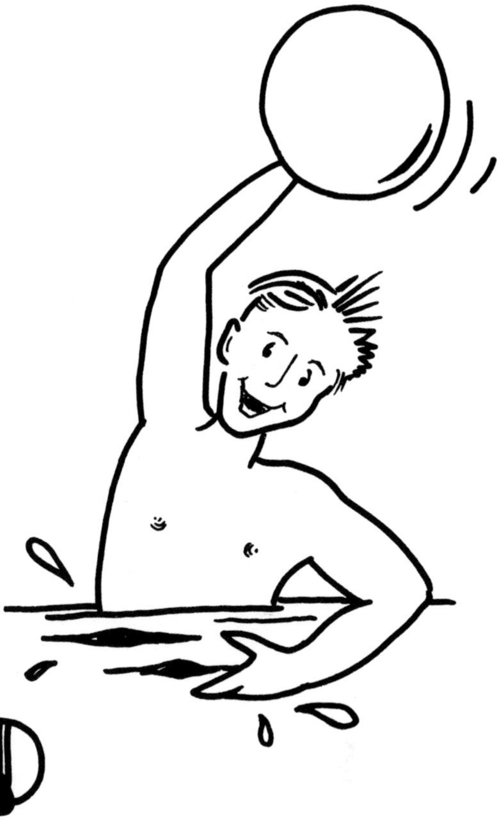

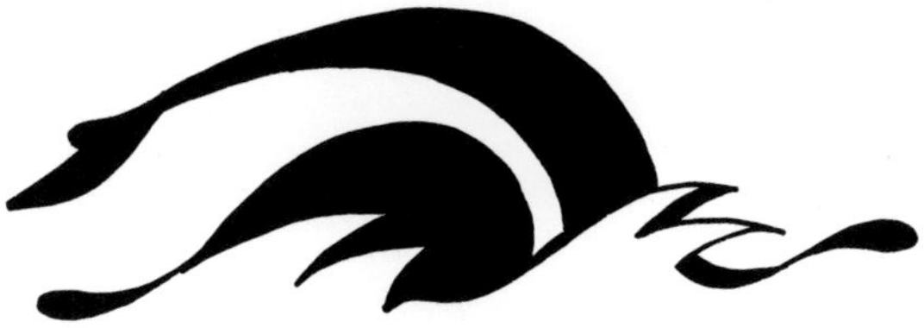

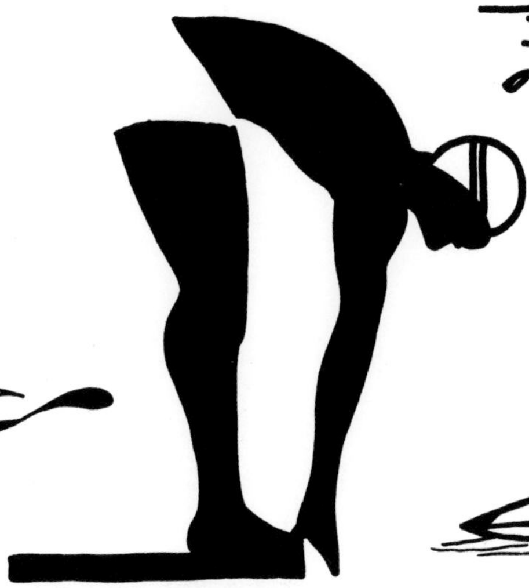

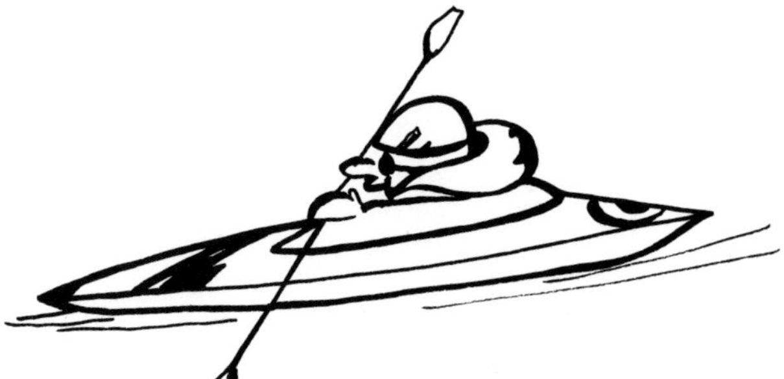

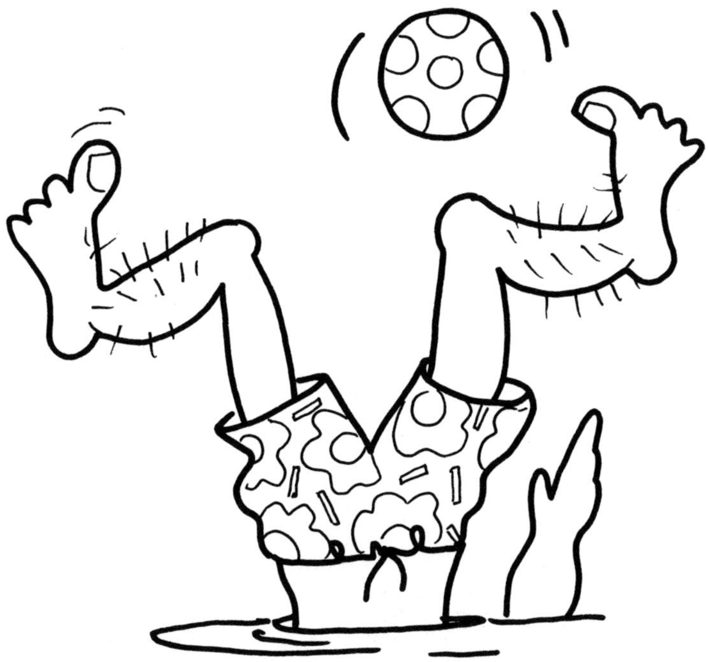

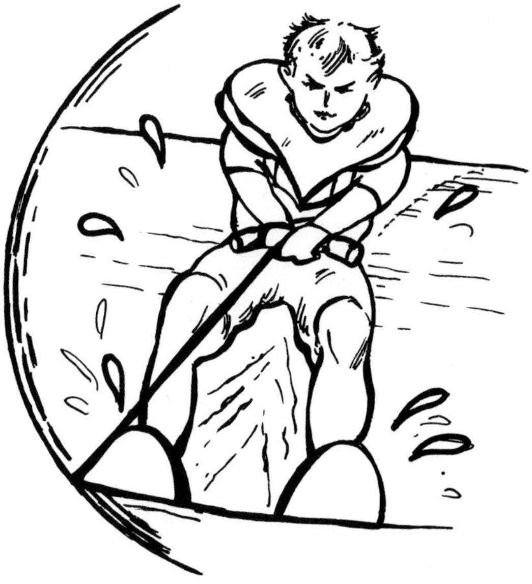

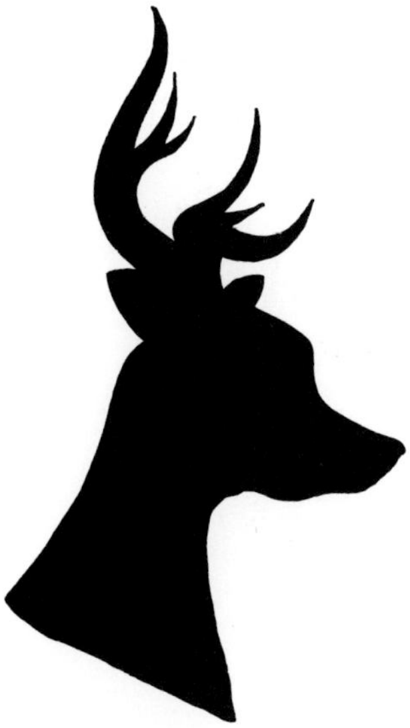

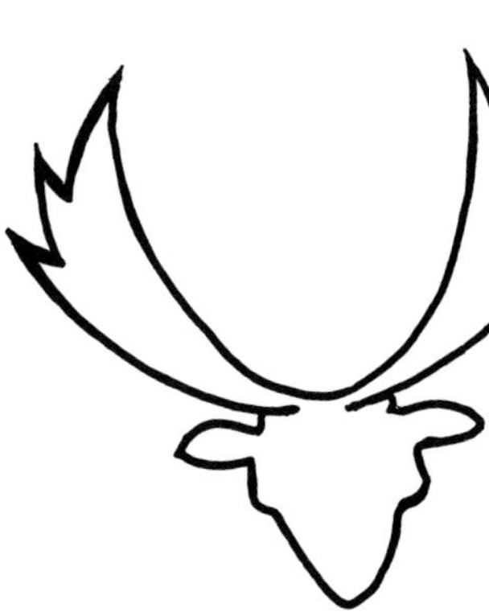

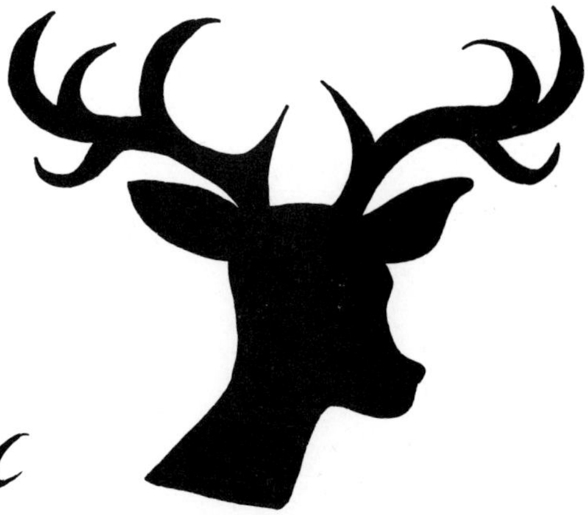

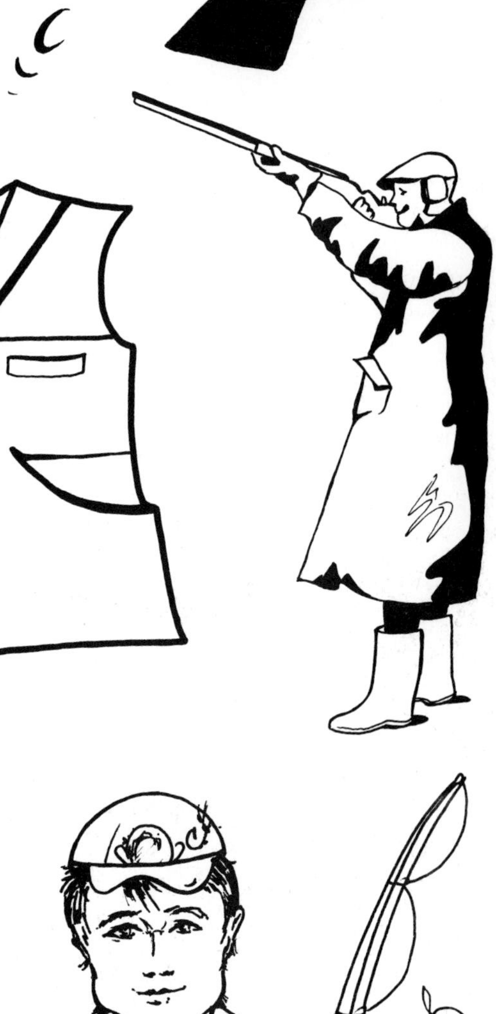

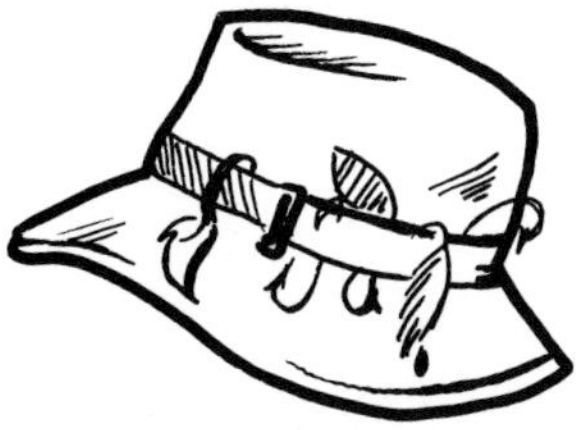

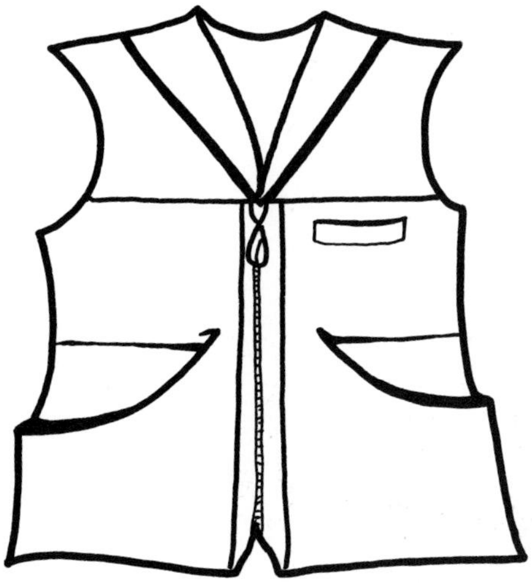

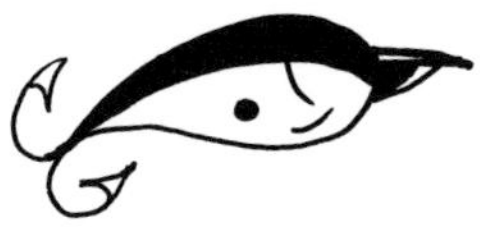

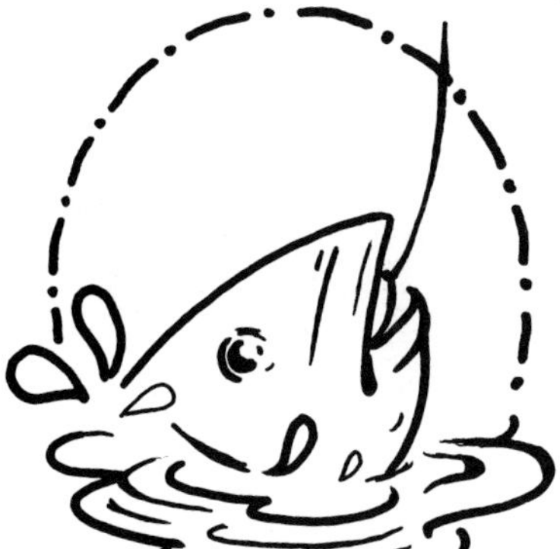

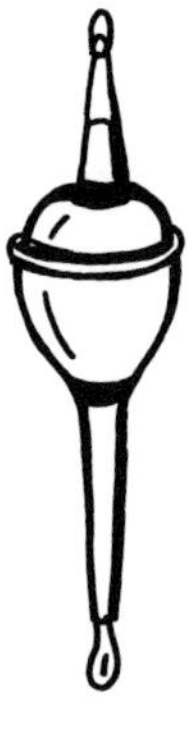

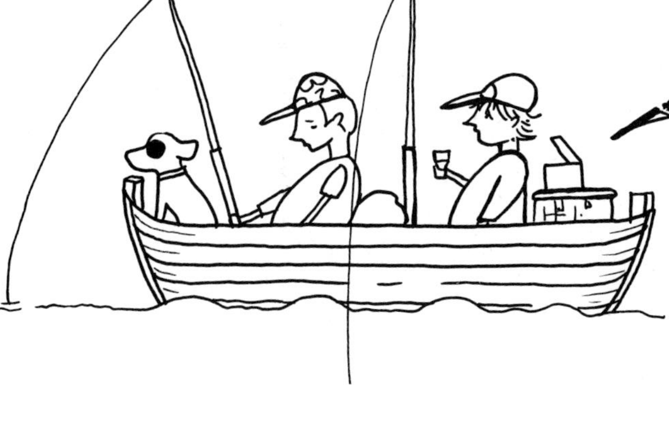

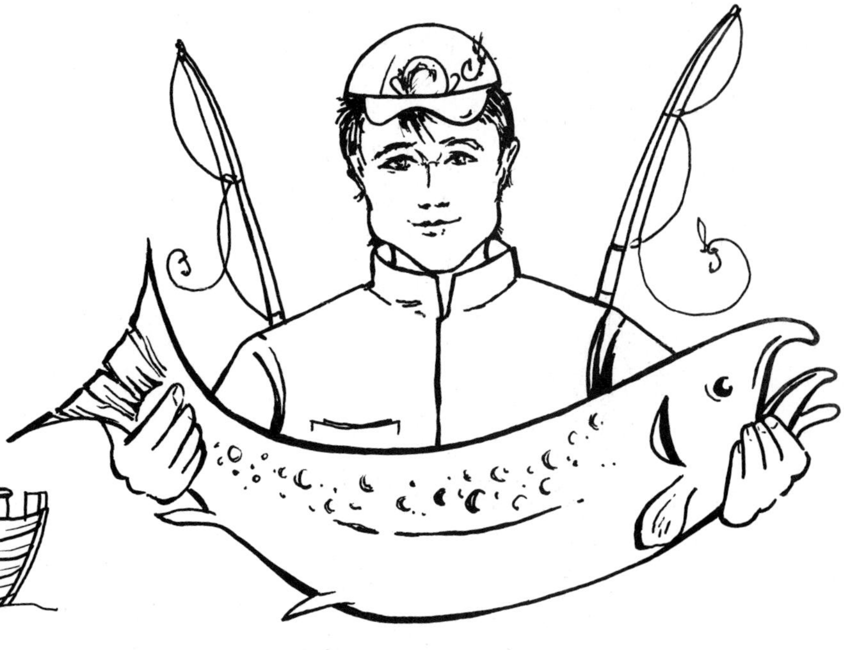

Transport

Planes, trains and automobiles are beloved of men the world over. Men and motors go together like ducks and water, and so no book on masculine motifs would be complete without a chapter dedicated to their favourite forms of transport.

This section starts with some exciting extra-terrestrial flying machines for those fired up by the great space race, but then comes back down to earth and out to sea with a selection of nautical-themed icons, which have been used to great effect on the items on page 24.

Revving up, pages 50–51 contain a great selection of cars, including the original Beetle, the Great British Taxi, classic sports cars, Formula 1 racing cars, cartoon-style cars and (love them or hate them) caravans.

Both the old days of steam and more modern locomotives are celebrated on pages 52–53, while air travel is the subject of pages 54–55. Heavy-duty vehicles such as lorries, tractors and construction giants round up the chapter, giving you a myriad of motifs to help you motor through your craft makes with ease.

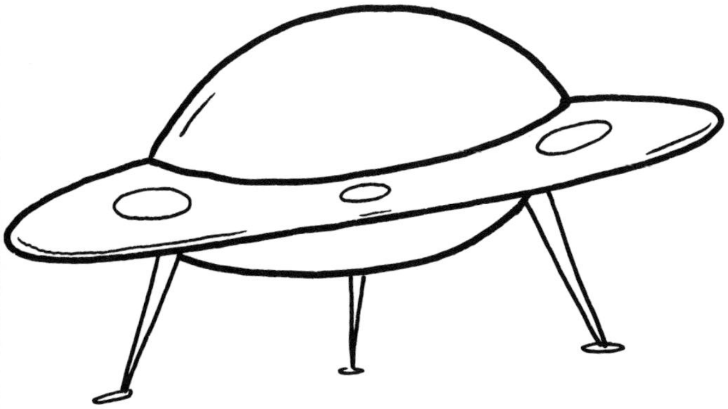

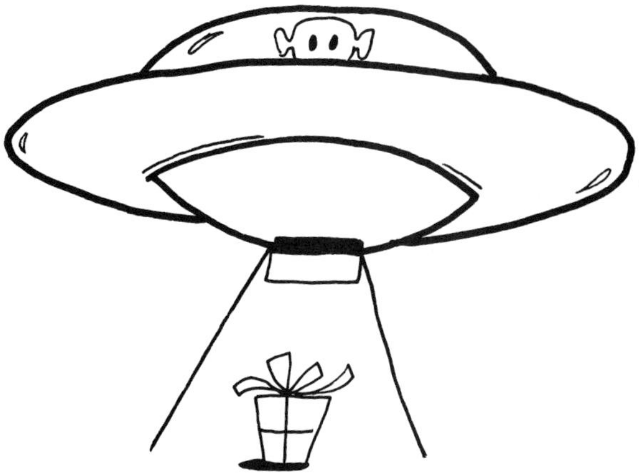

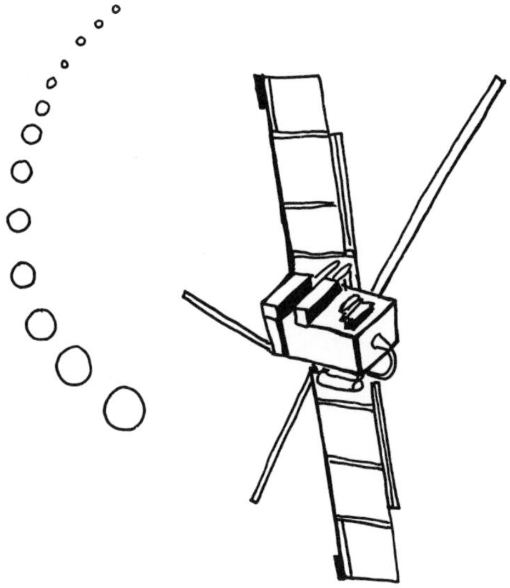

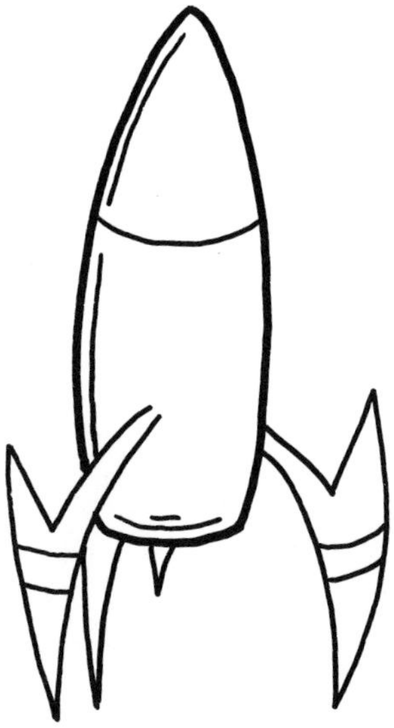

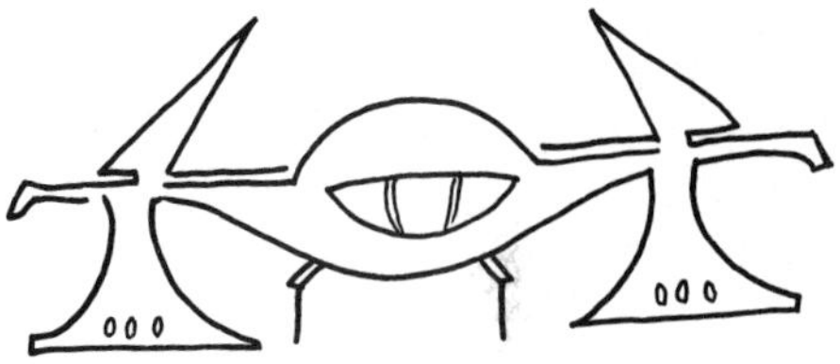

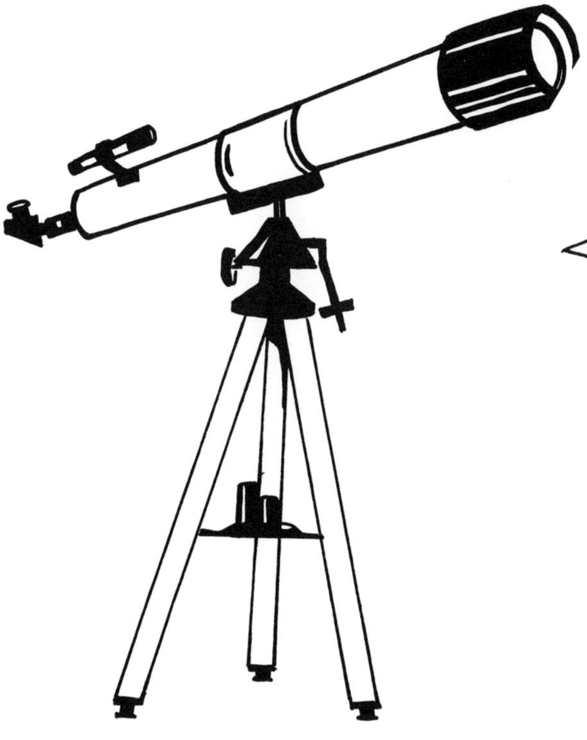

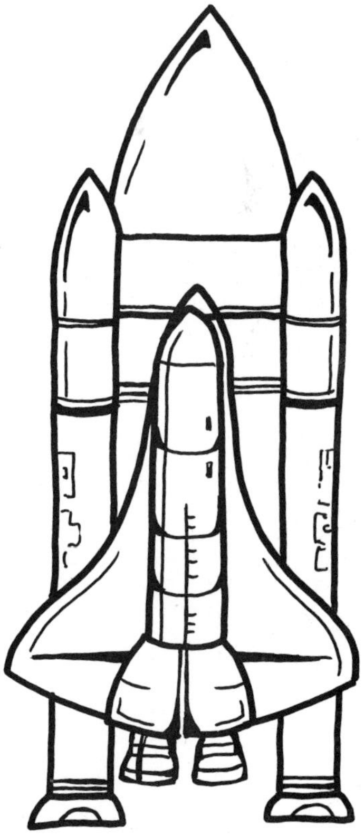

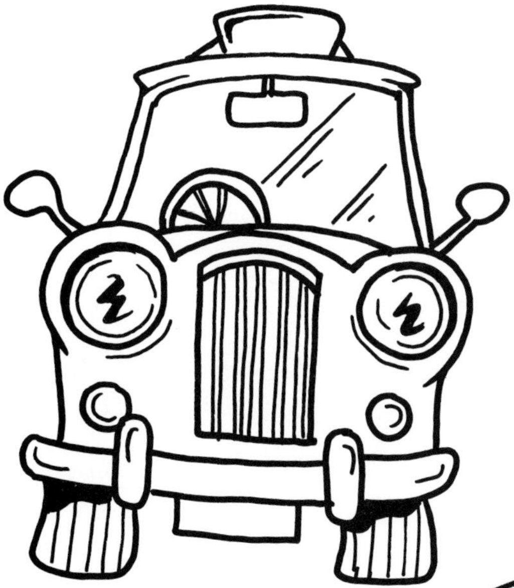

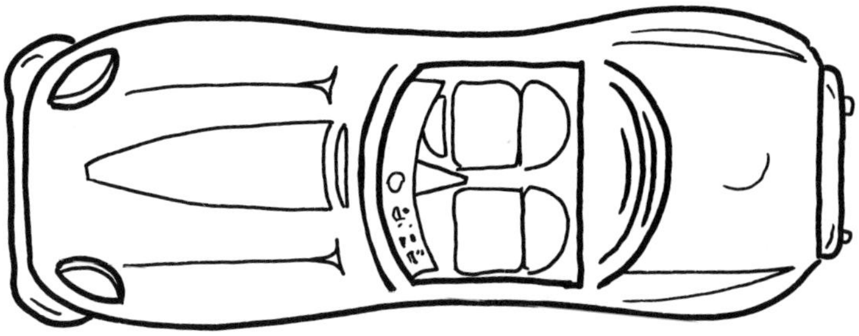

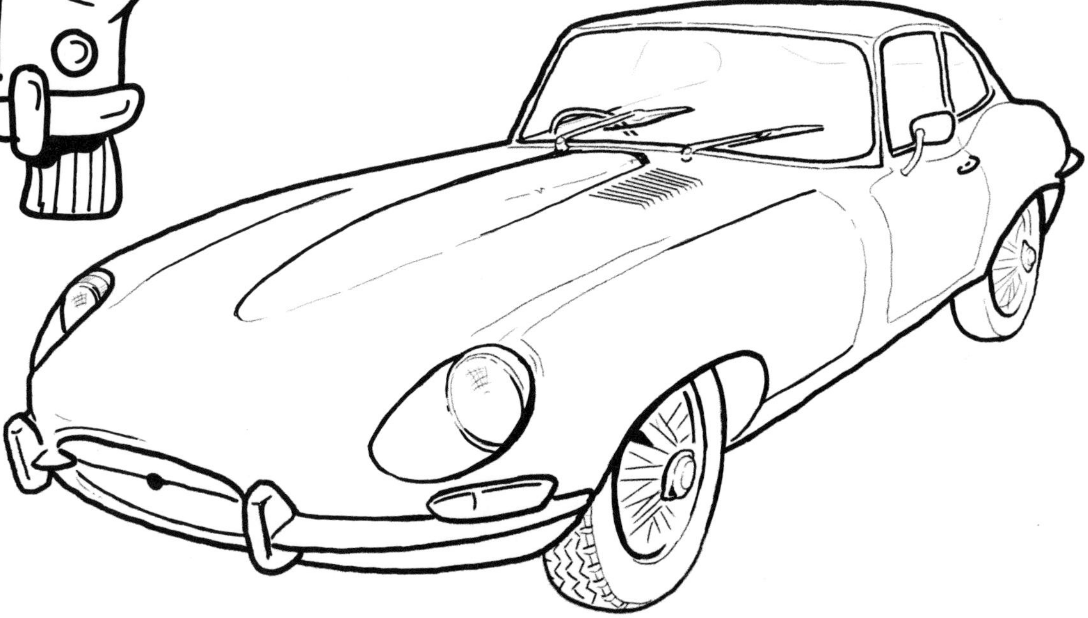

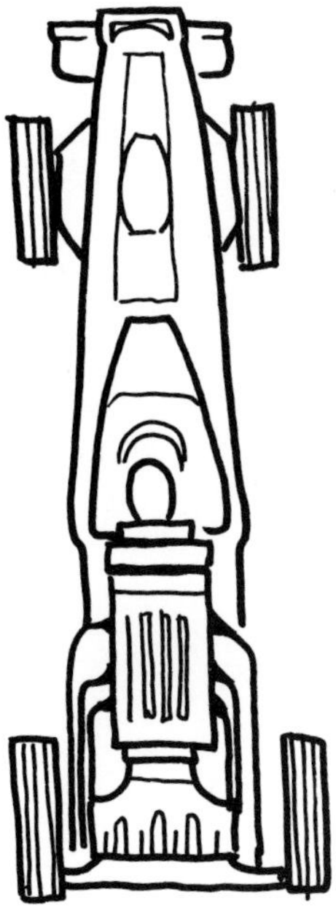

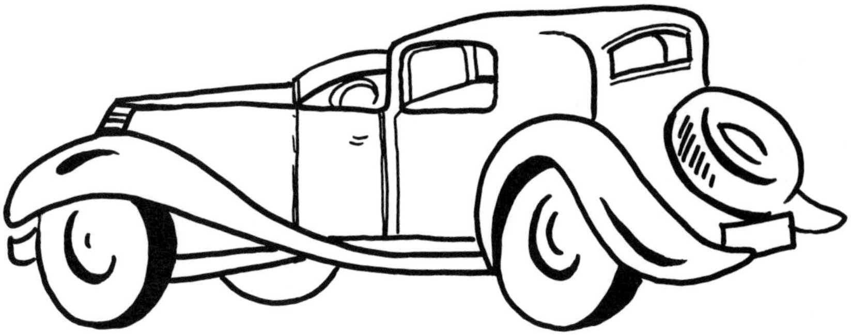

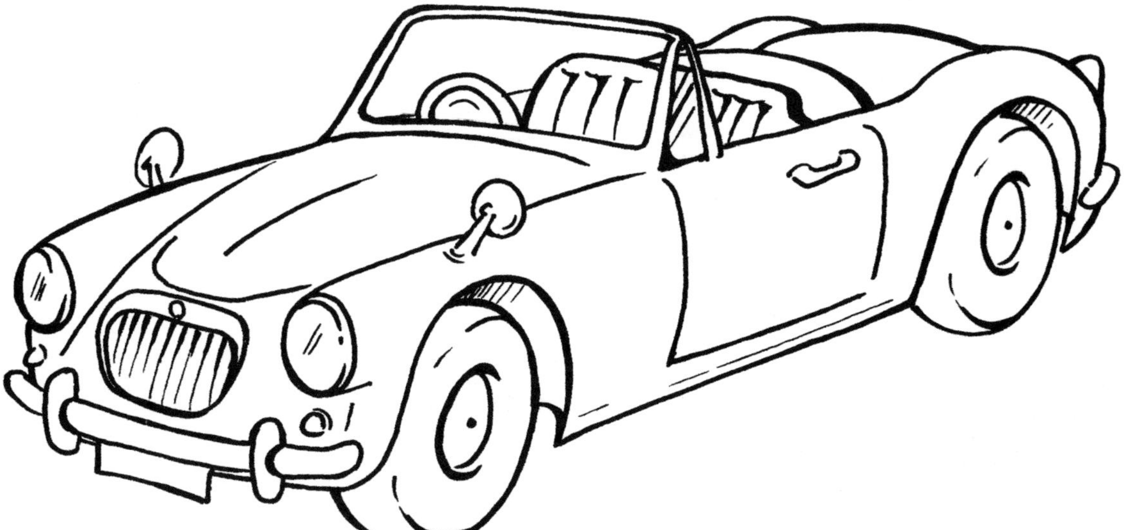

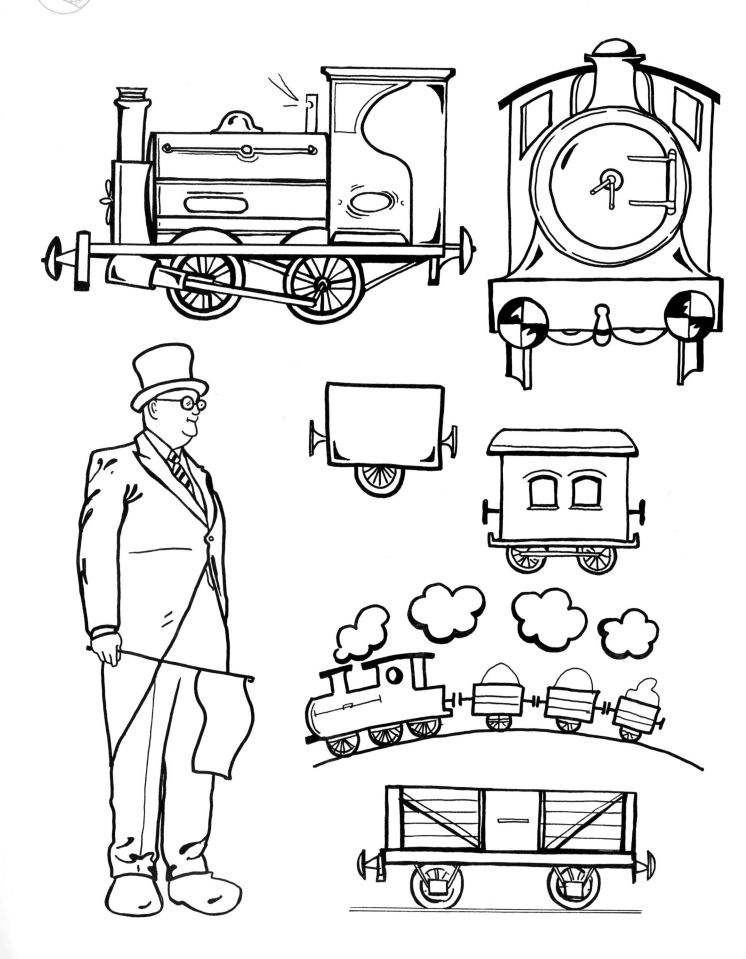

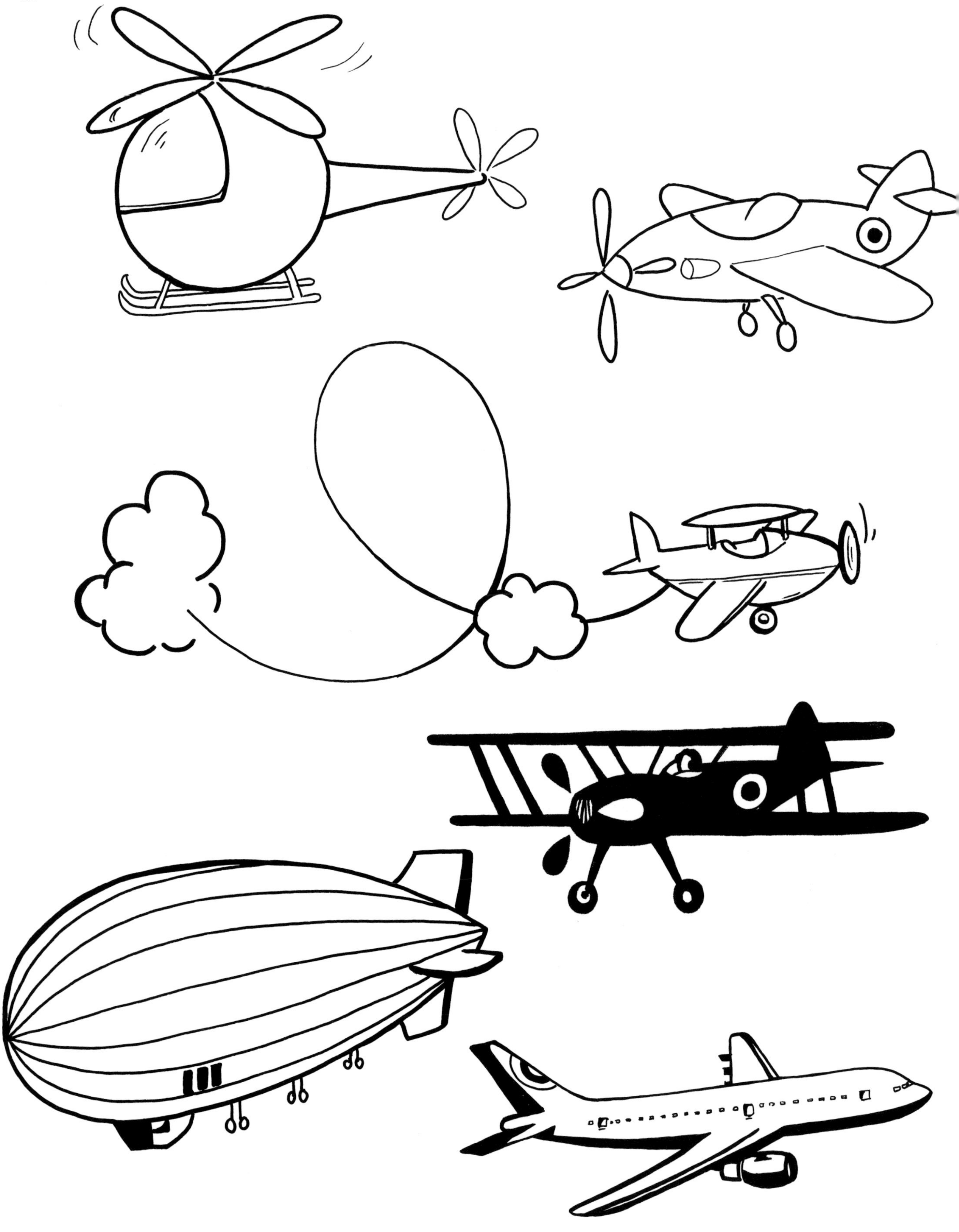

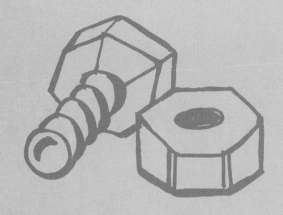

Working life

The world of work is almost endlessly variable, and it would be very difficult to include motifs for every single job here. However, this chapter covers most of the major professions, and gives many useful emblems for things men may like to do in their spare time too, such as do-it-yourself and motor mechanics.

Starting with the daily routine of shaving and dressing, the chapter moves on to the tools of the trade and some DIY essentials, including painting and decorating, plumbing and general maintenance. See the cards on pages 14, 15 and 20 for ideas on how to use these motifs.

A plethora of trades are covered on pages 64–65, from scientist to dentist, postman to fireman, broker to butcher and more.

If motors are his trade or his passion, there are motifs galore on pages 66–67, and working vehicles including buses, emergency vehicles and tractors follow on pages 68–69.

Finally, a career in the military, or a stint in the TA, can be illustrated using one of the many motifs on pages 70–71.

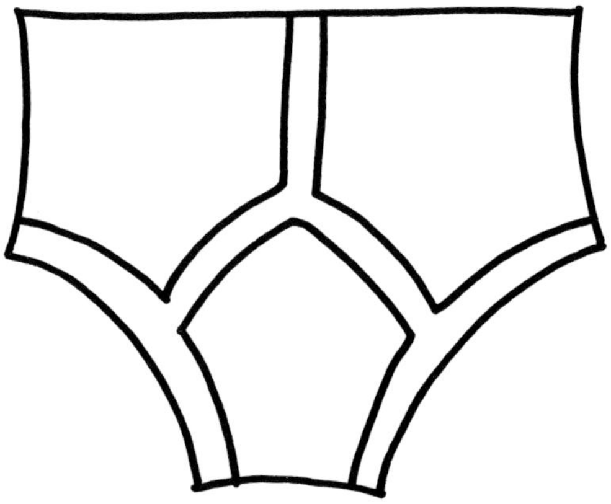

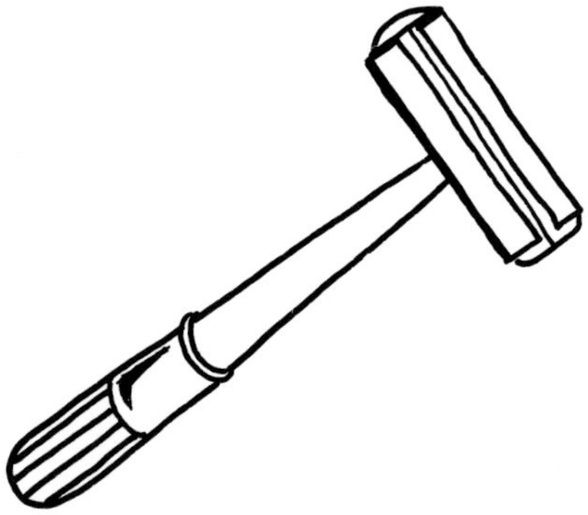

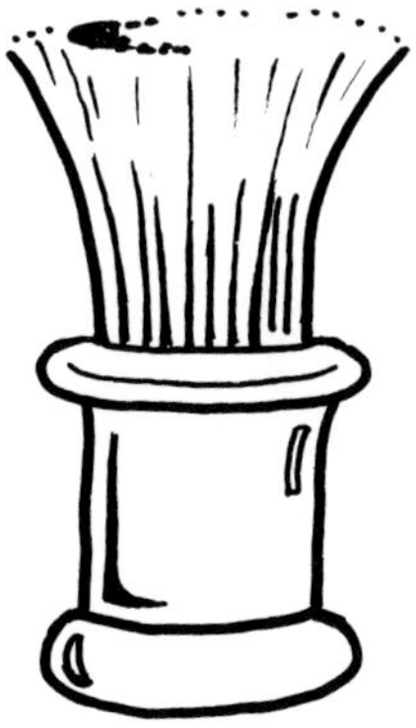

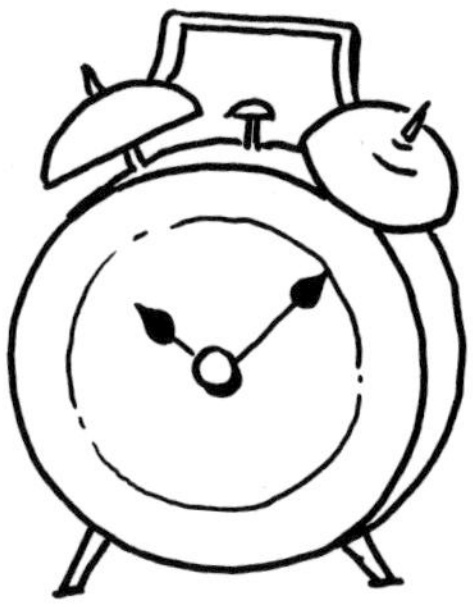

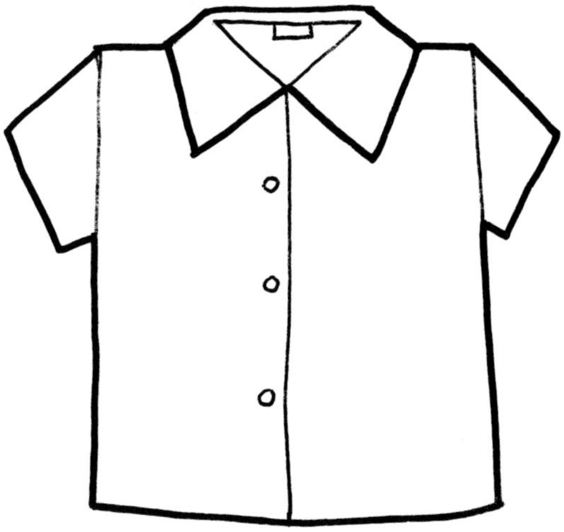

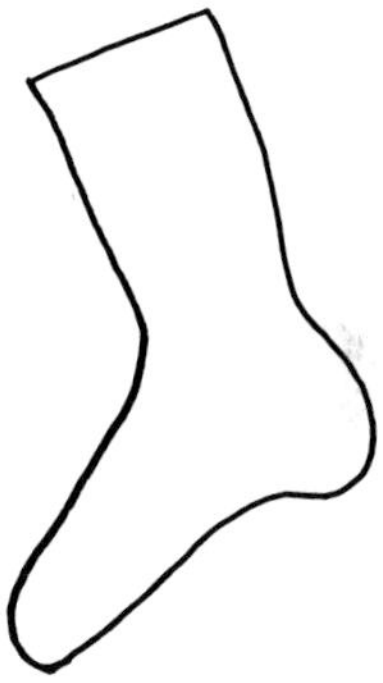

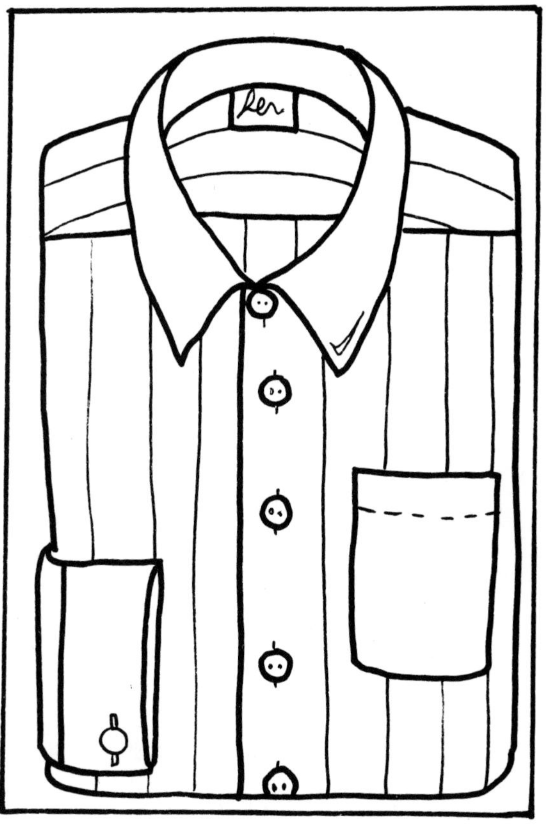

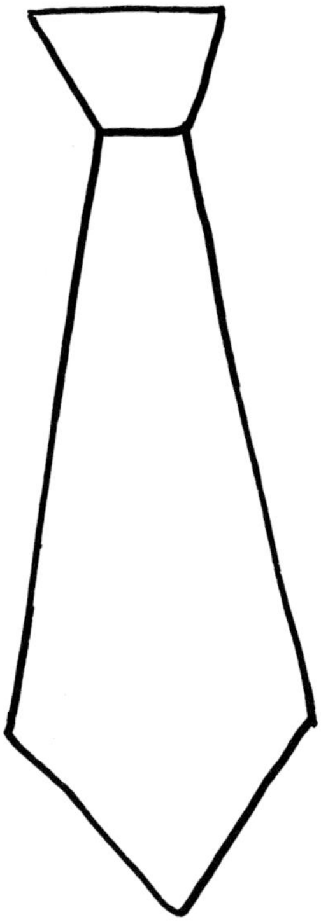

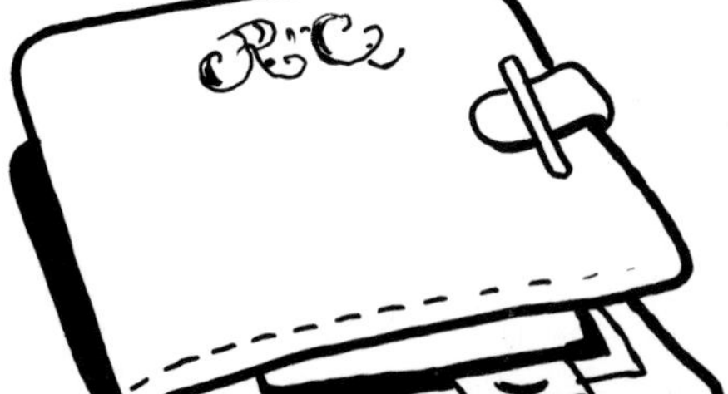

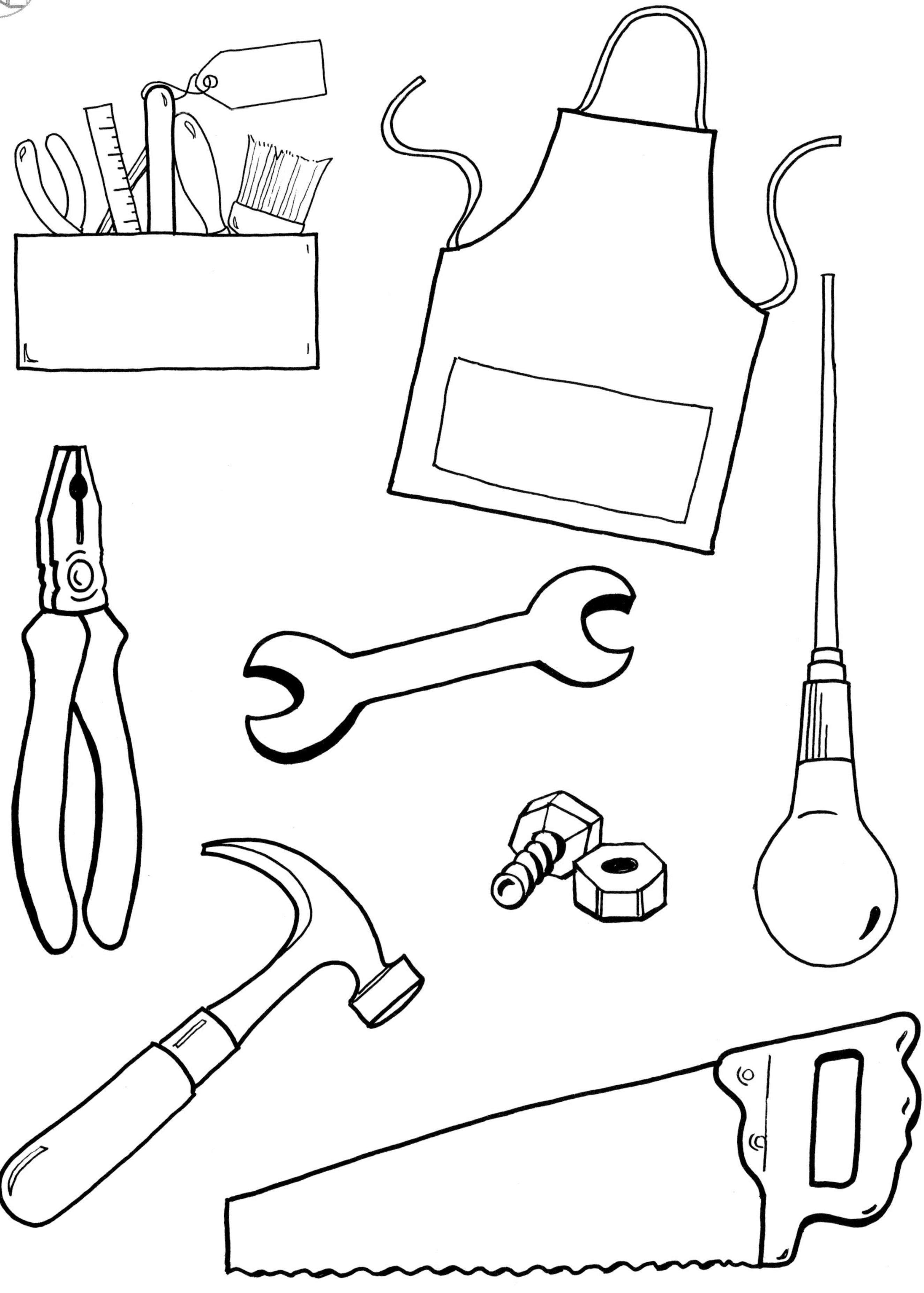

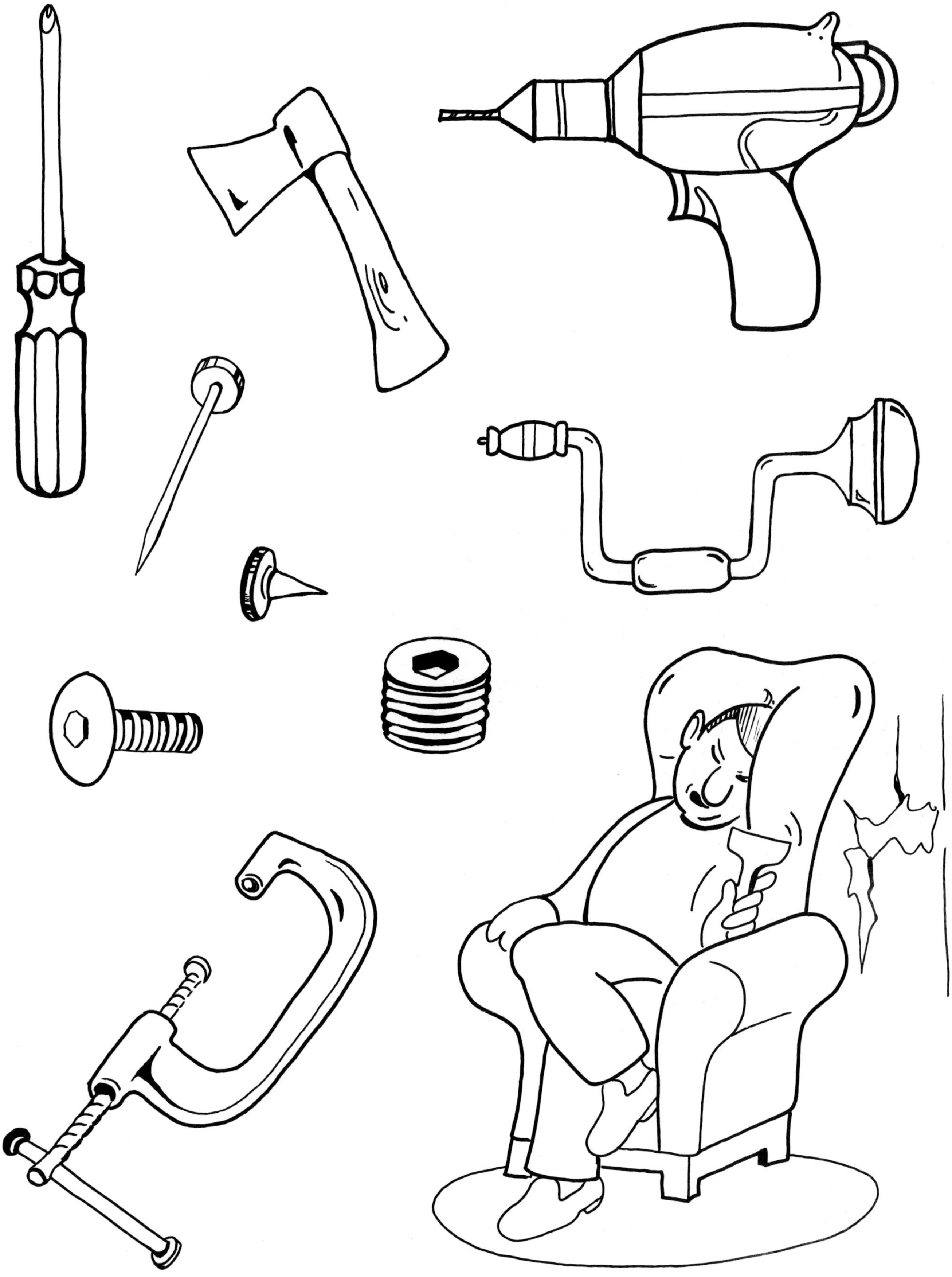

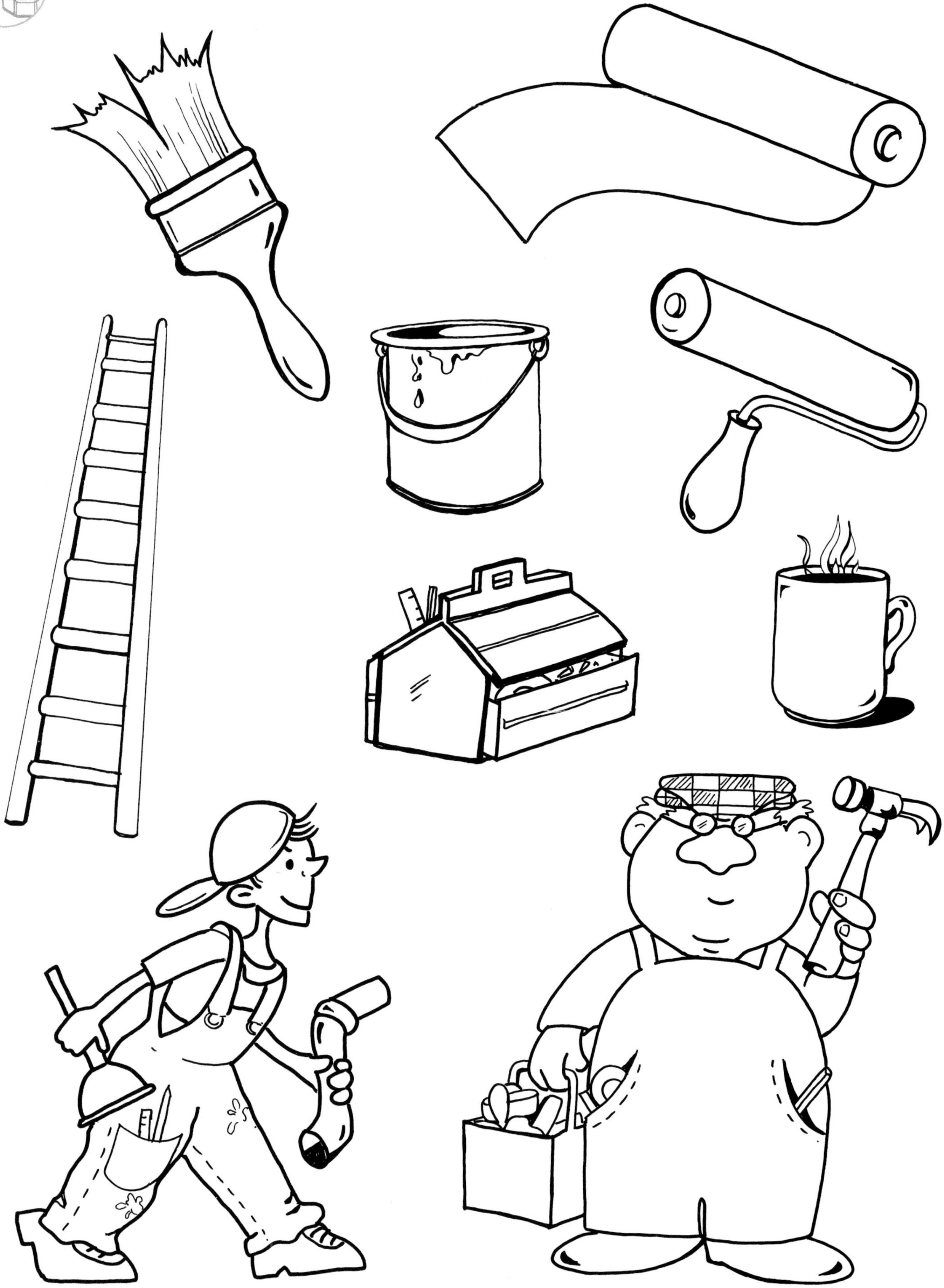

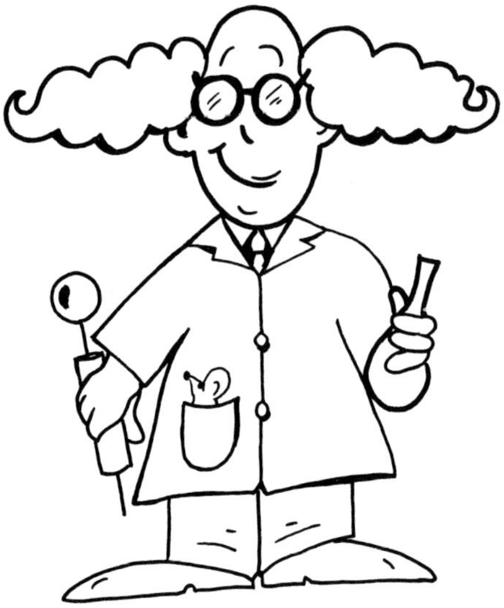

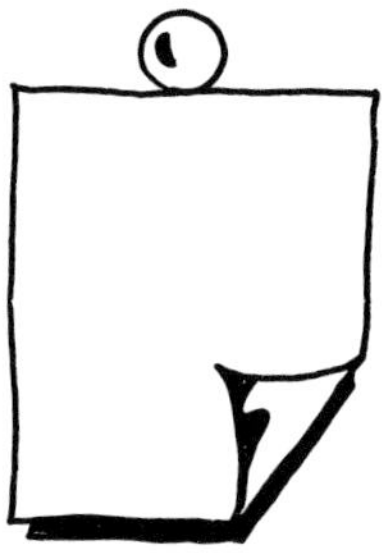

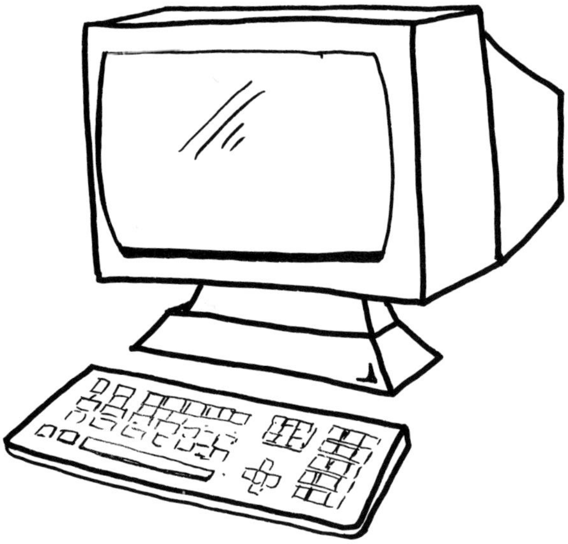

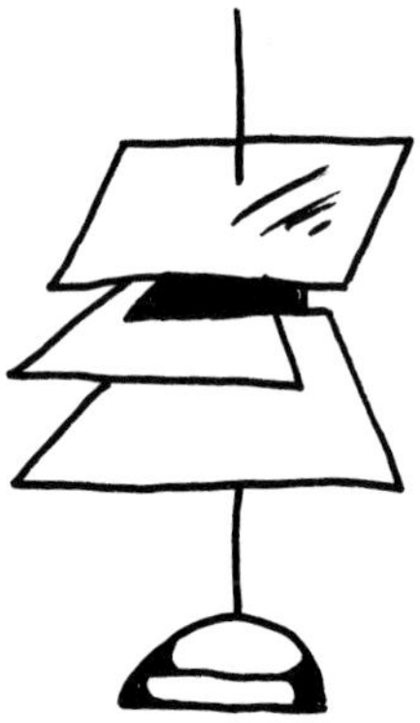

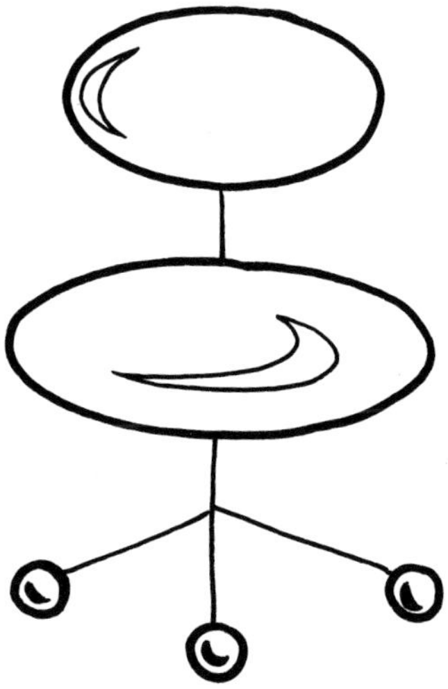

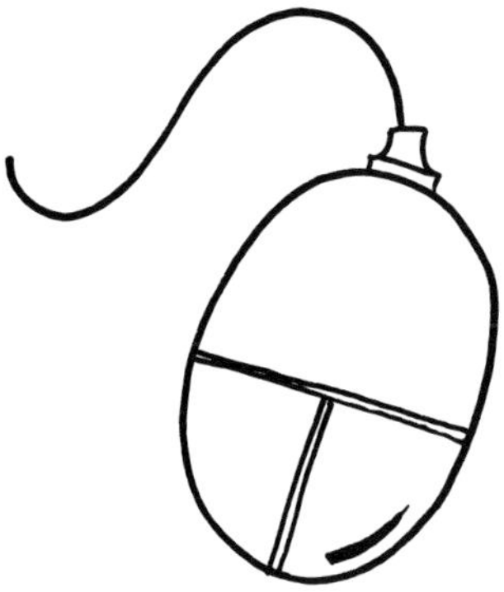

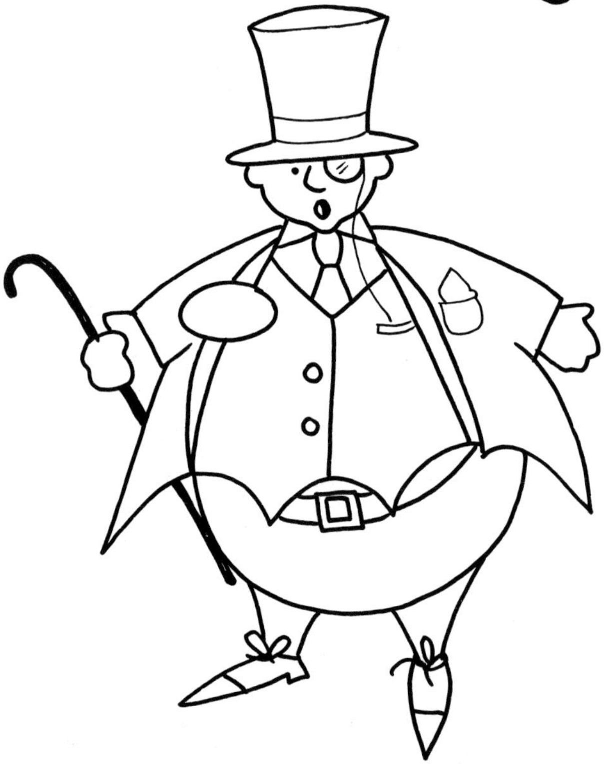

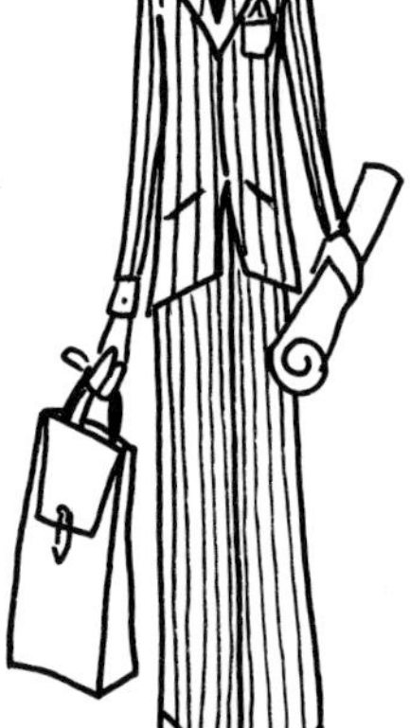

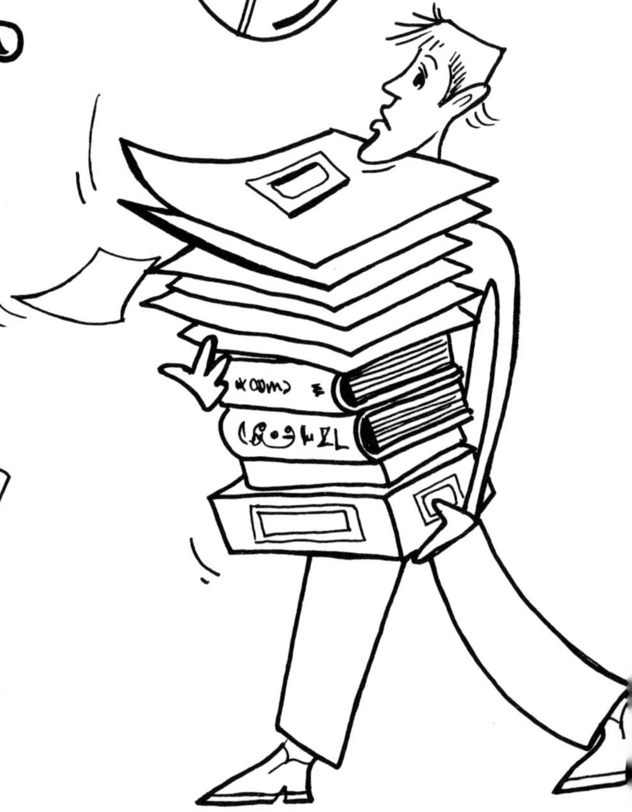

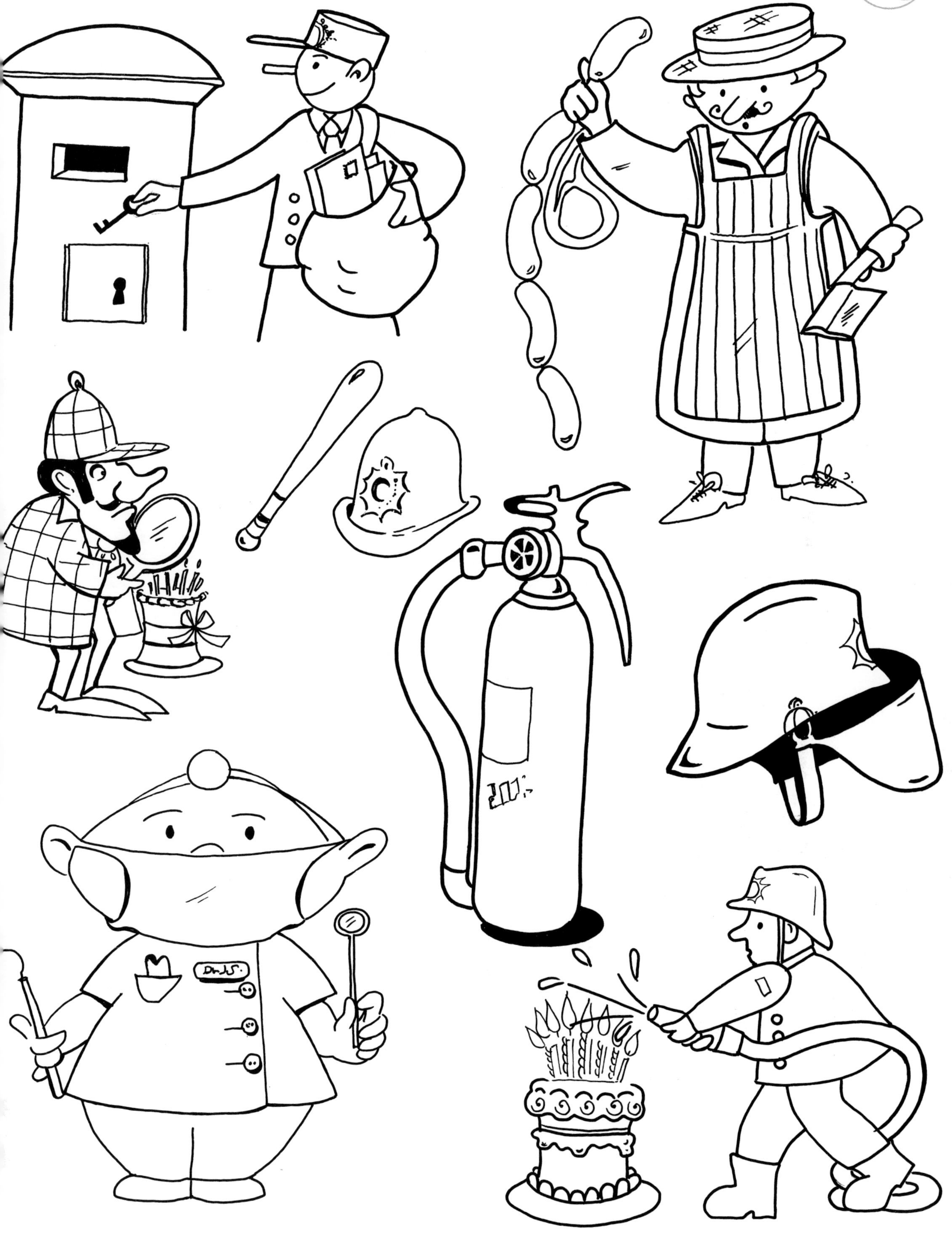

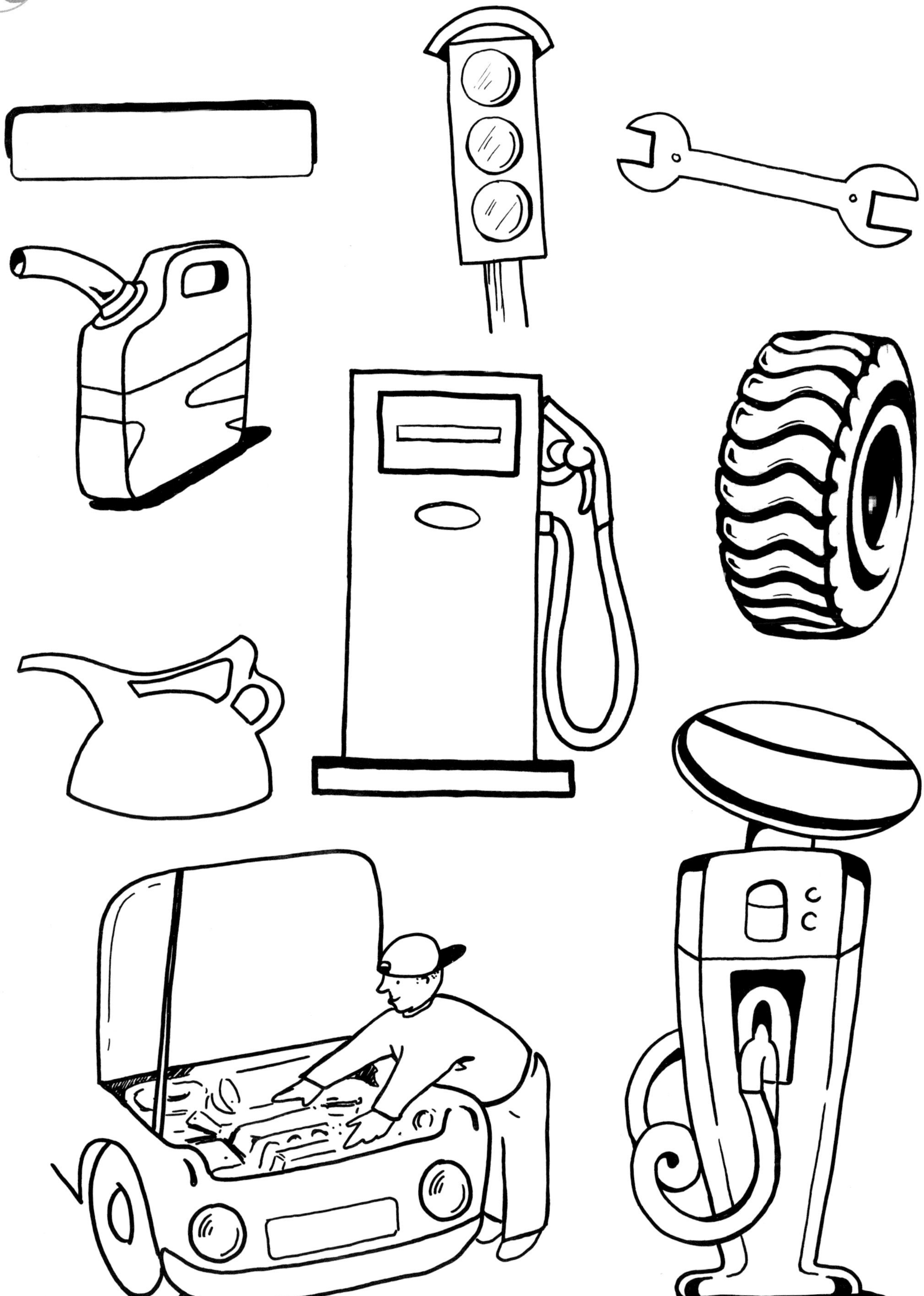

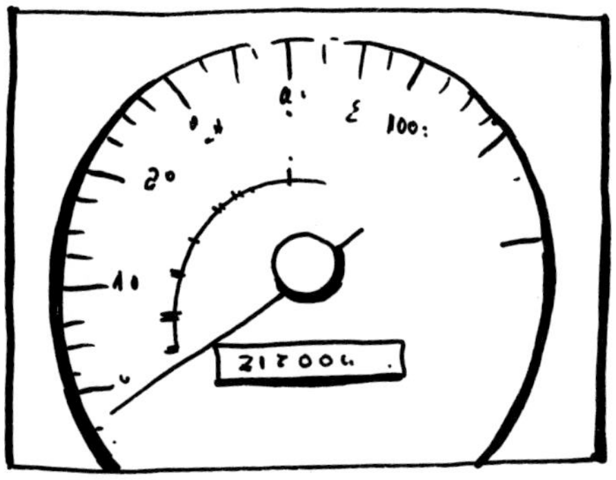

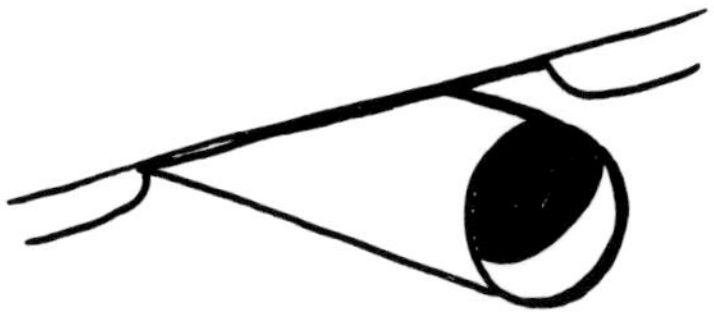

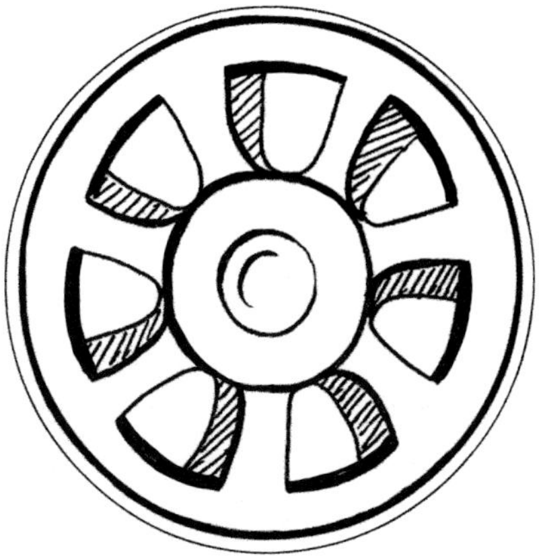

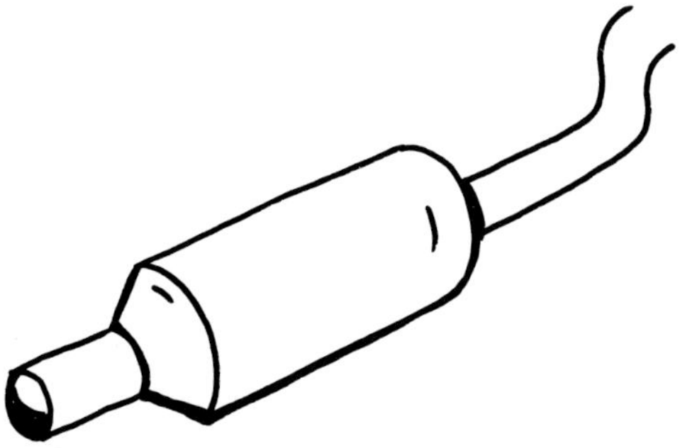

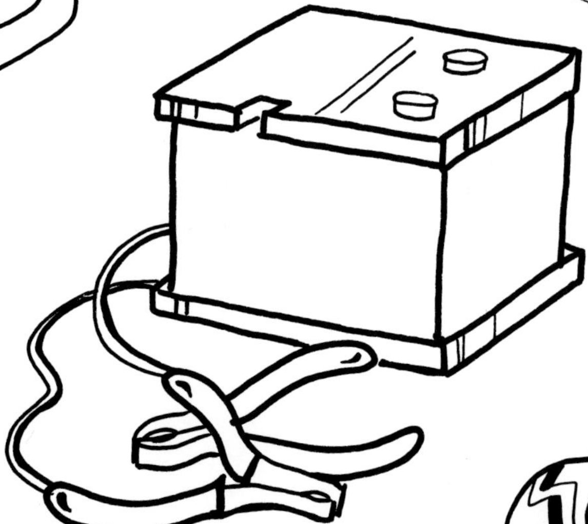

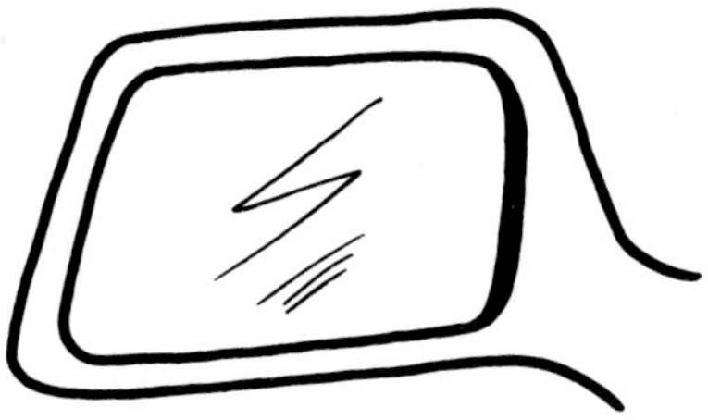

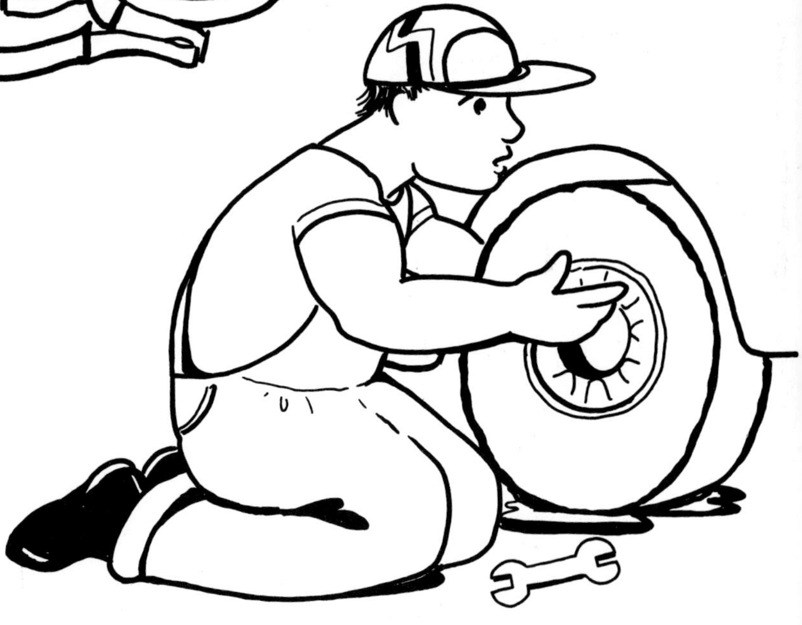

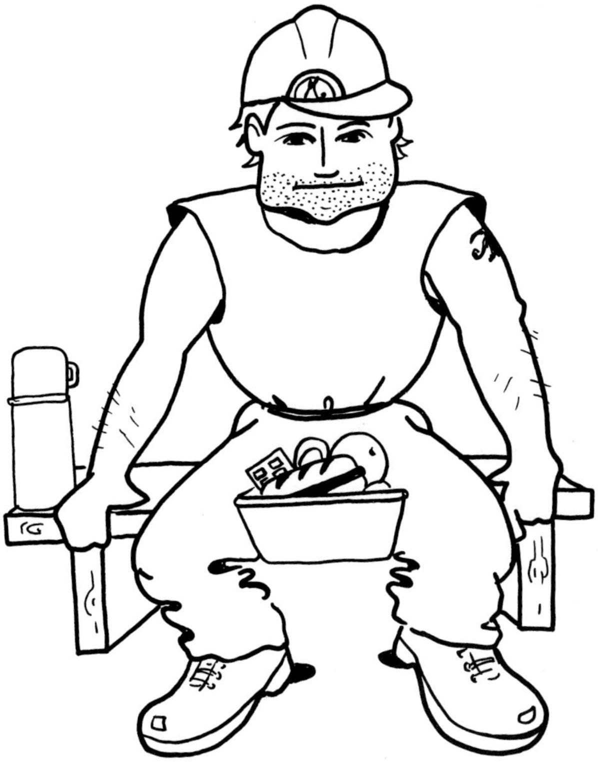

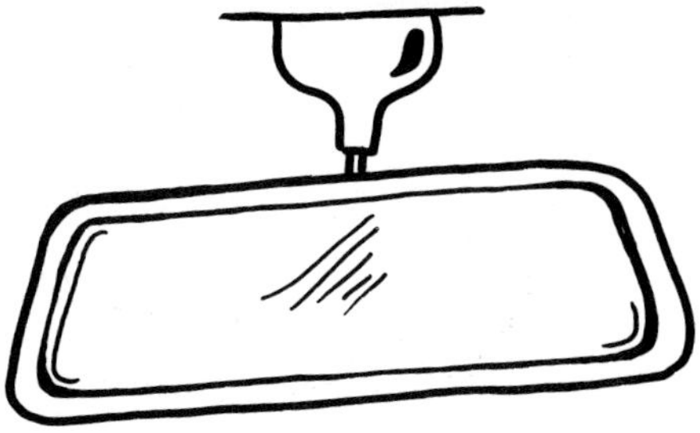

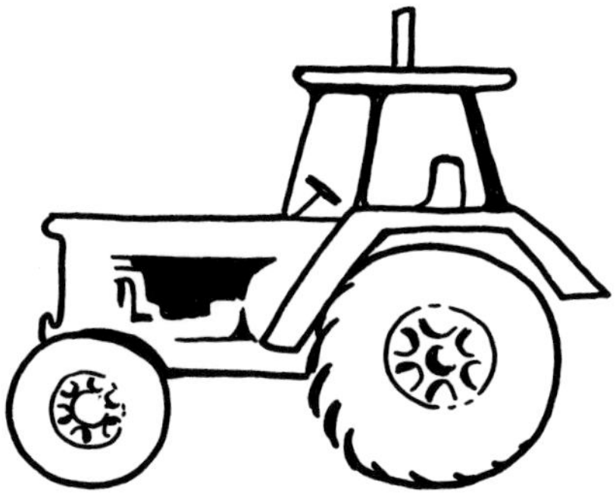

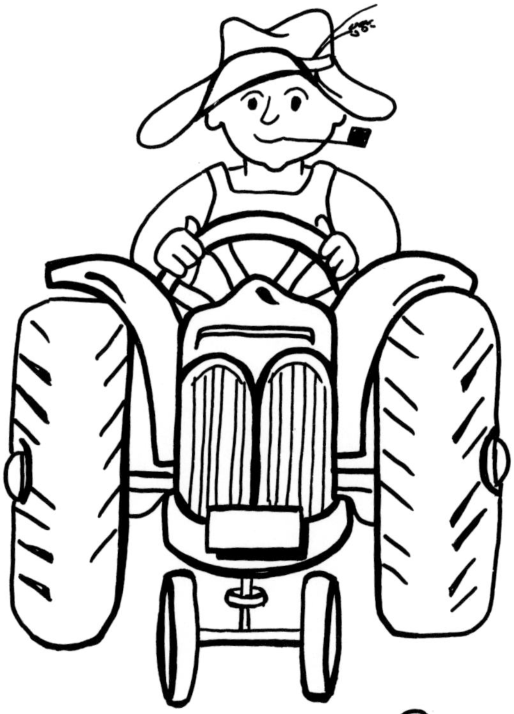

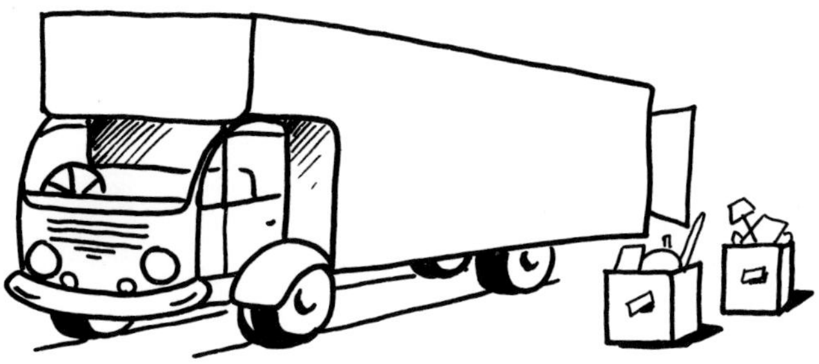

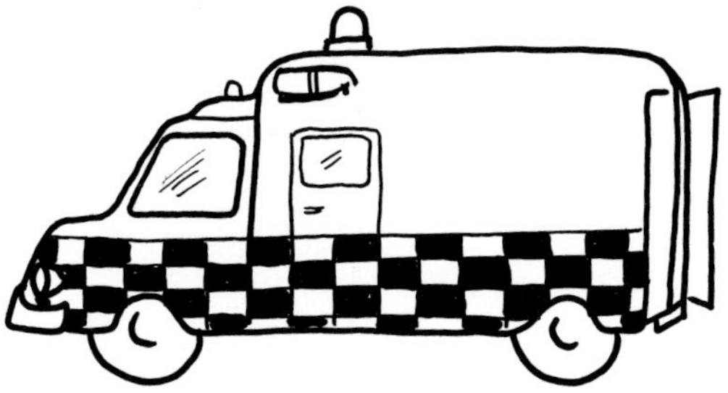

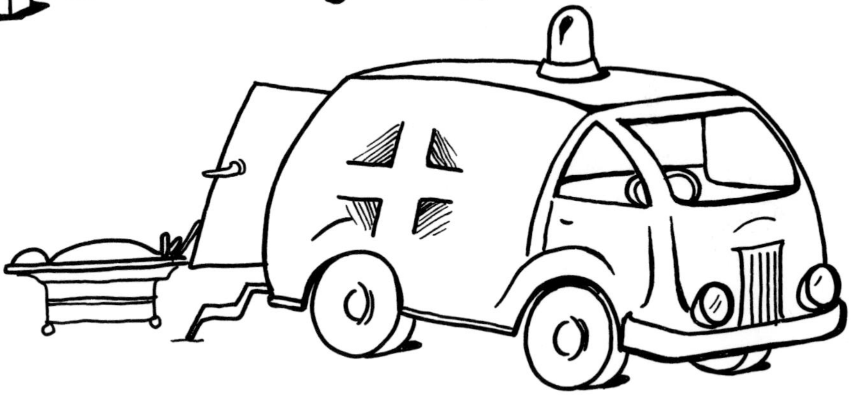

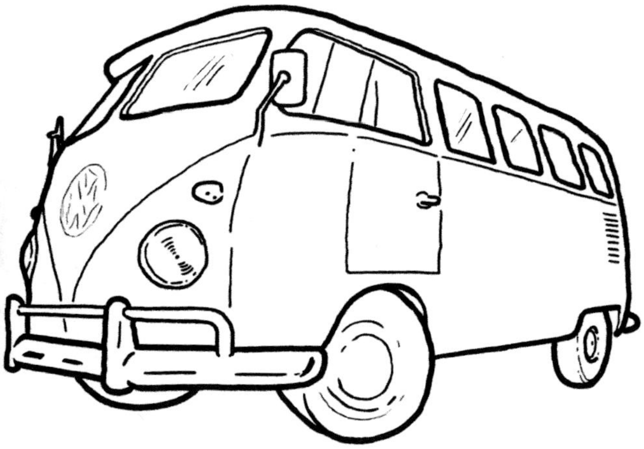

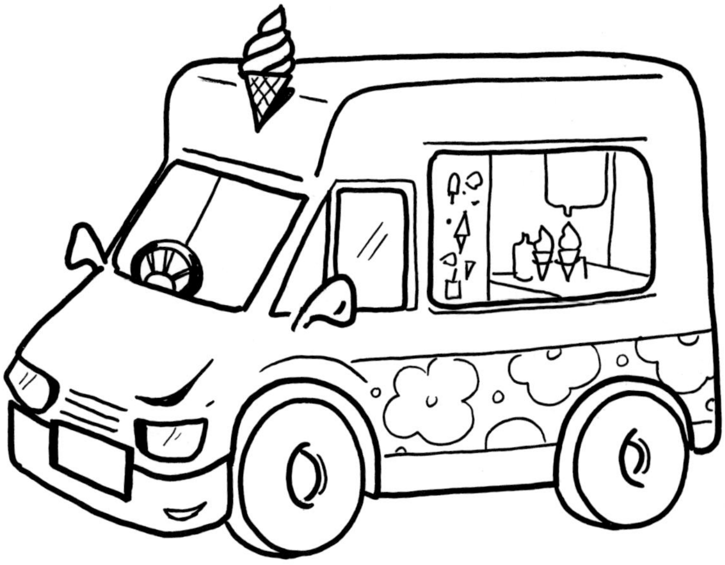

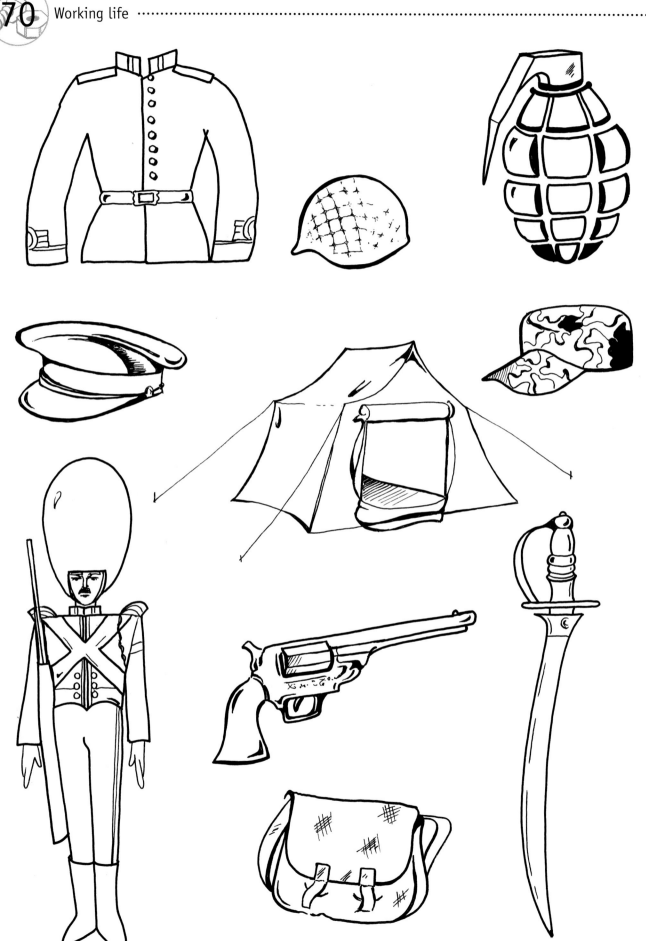

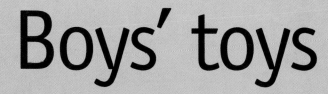

Boys' toys

Boys will be boys ... and this means that no matter how old they get, they will never stop their fun and games. This chapter looks at some of the things men do to enjoy themselves, and focuses on the hardware in particular.

Whether it's performing a solo concerto, or rocking the mic in a punk band, the motifs shown opposite are a great place to start for all the male maestros in your life.

Drinking is usually quite high on most men's list of relaxation techniques, and the motifs on pages 74–75 will help you show this in your craft projects.

What man doesn't love technological gadgets? From the latest plasma-screen TV, to flashy mobile phones, sat-nav systems, MP3 players and games consoles – there is a wealth truly 'techy' motifs on pages 76–77.

If your man feels the need for speed, there enough motorbikes to please him on pages 78–79, while big boys who enjoy table football, paintballing, fruit machines and brain-training games are also catered for. So, bring on the fun – there is something here for everyone.

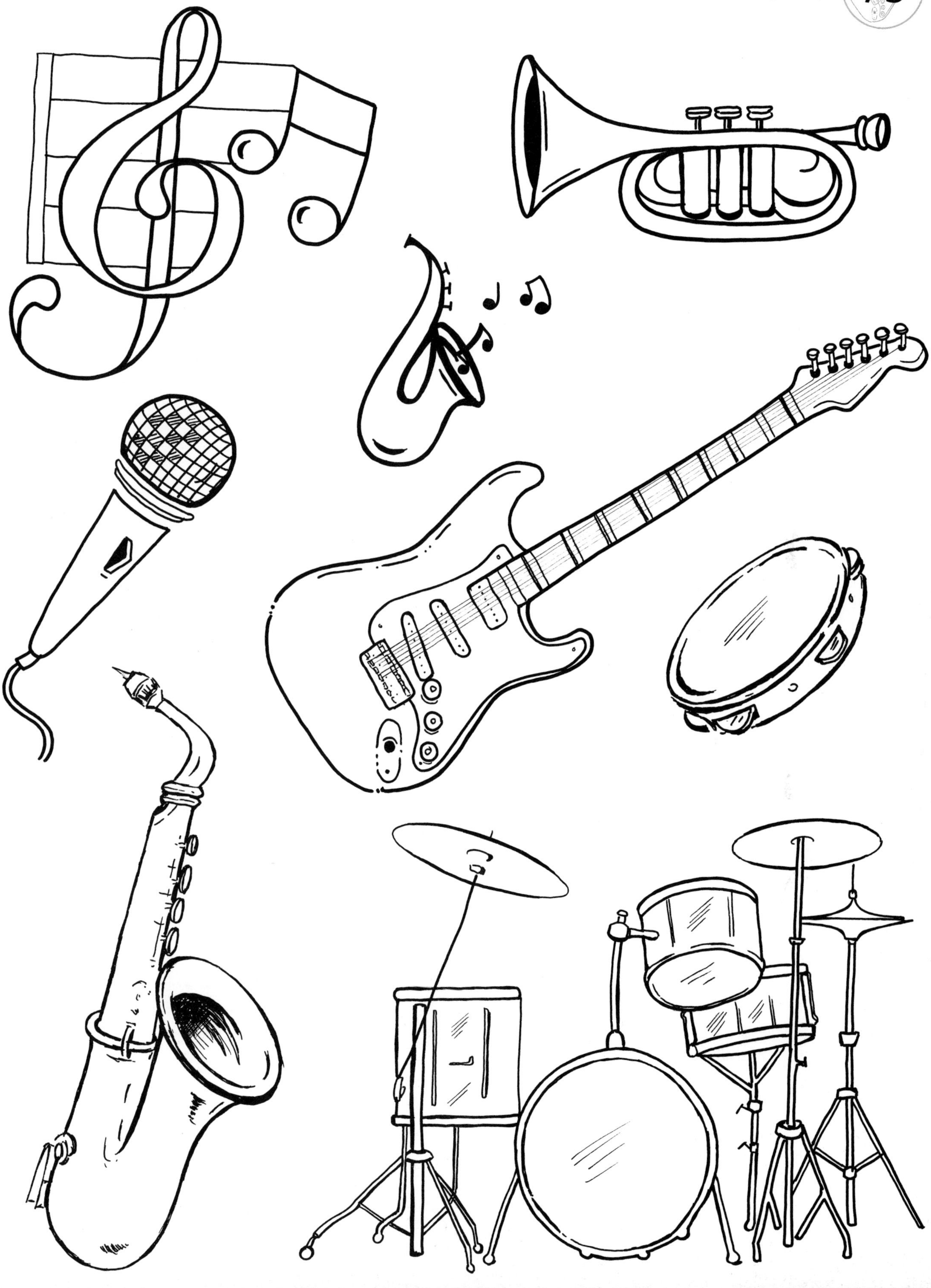

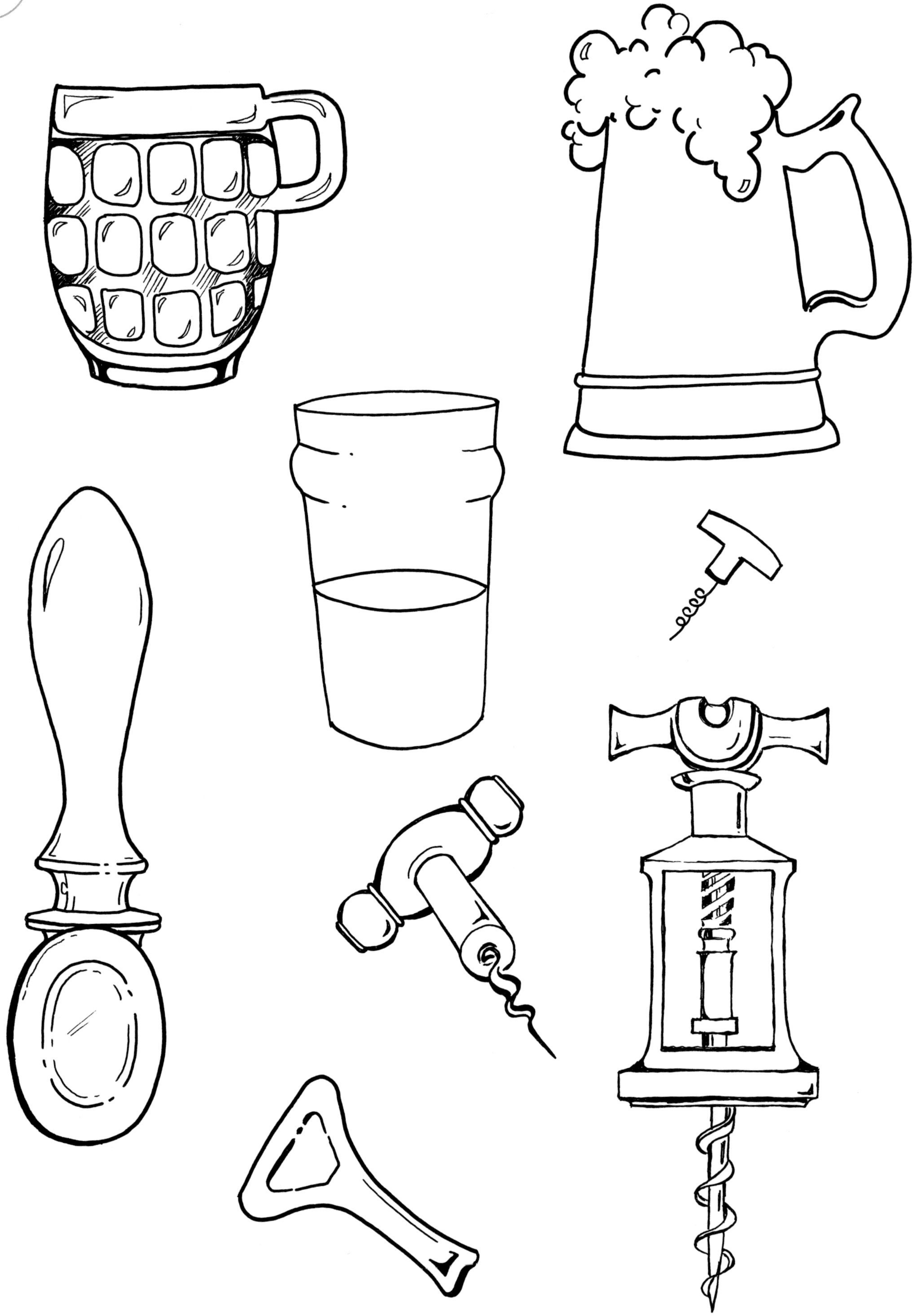

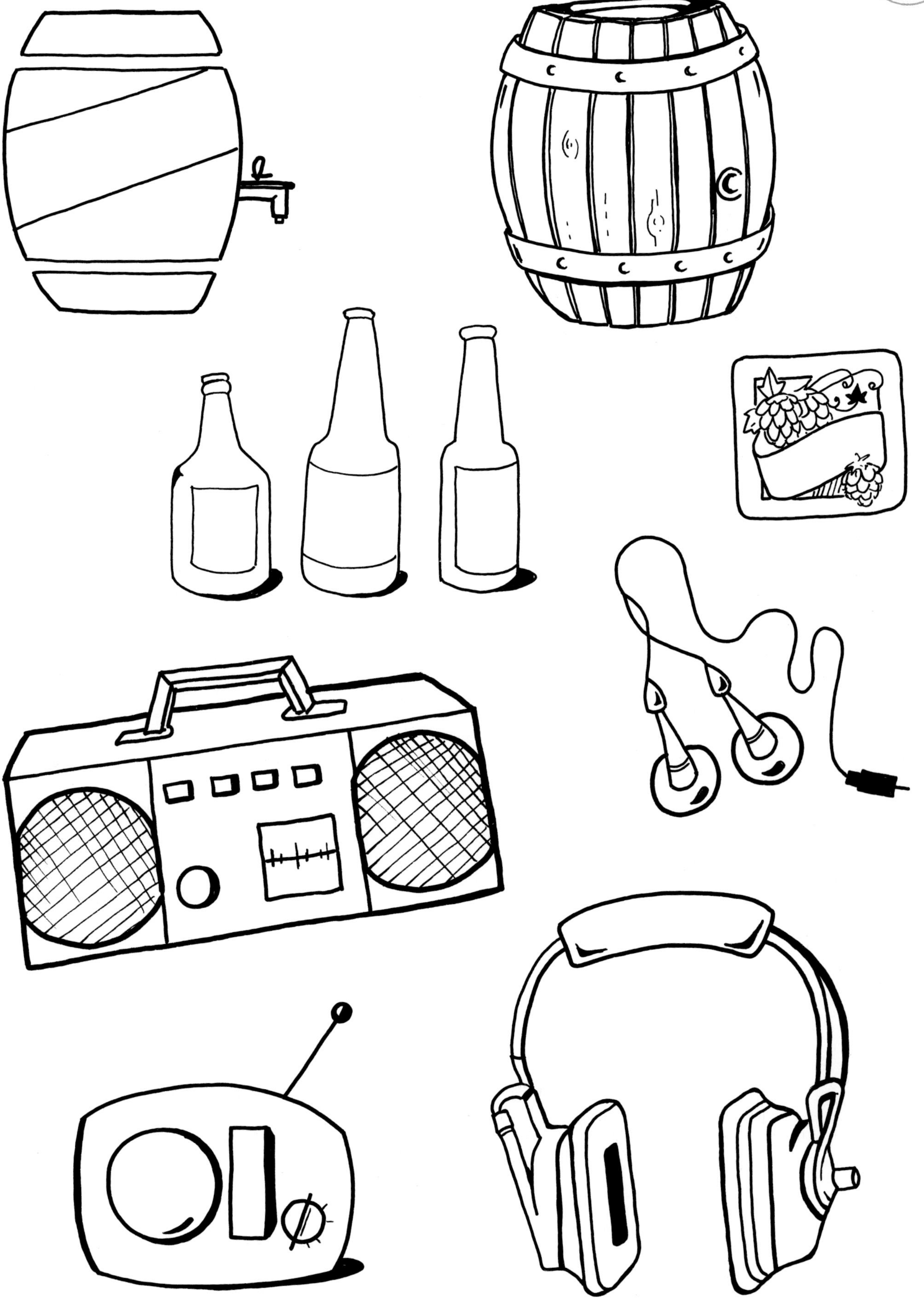

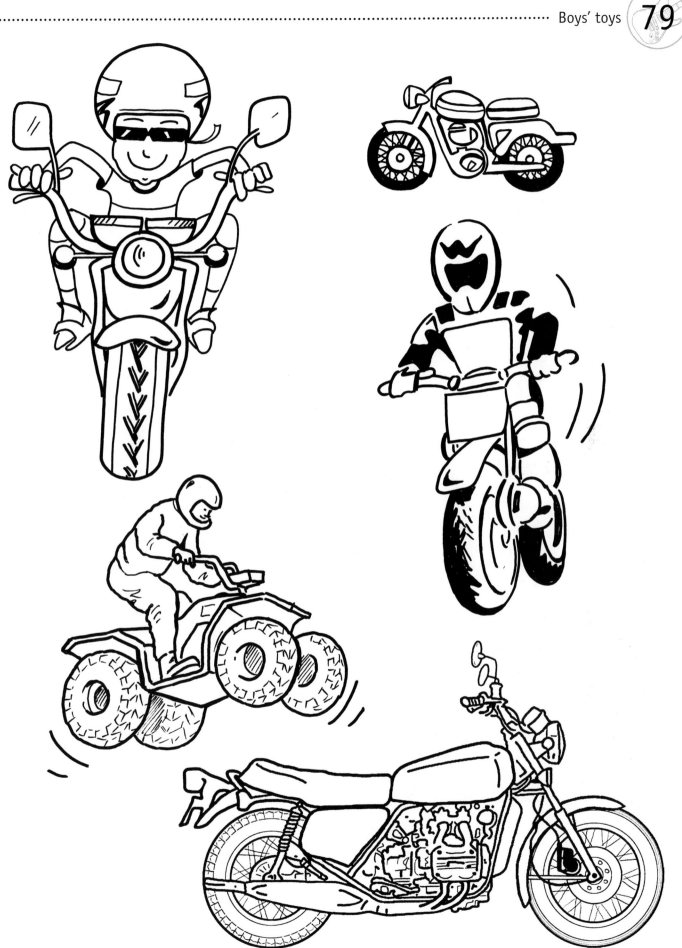

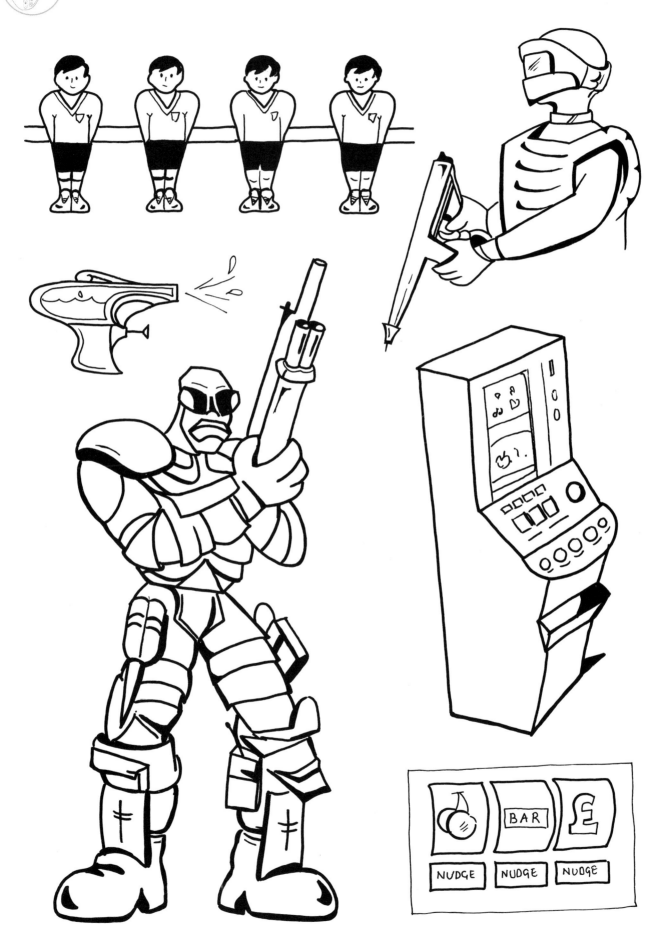

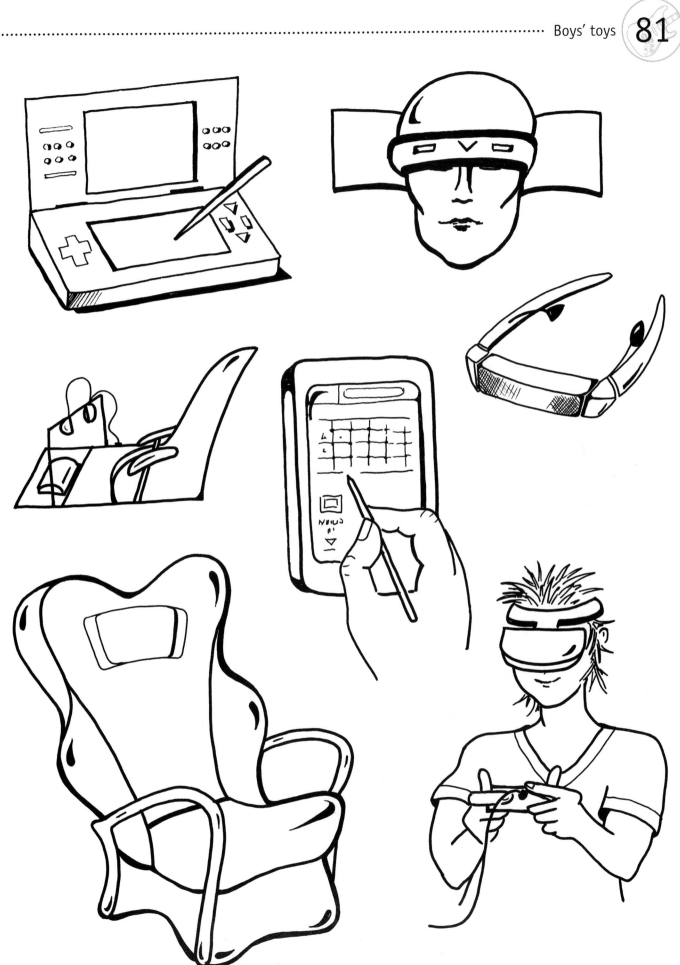

Occasions

Becoming a parent is a major event, but all too often the father is rather overlooked, as the mother receives the majority of the attention. To help redress the balance, this chapter starts with some great motifs to illustrate the coming of fatherhood.

As well as the birth of children, many other celebrations are also included here, such as birthdays, graduation, success at sport and passing the driving test, for which the car card shown on page 21 would be perfect.

Men being men, inevitably at some time or other an injury will occur, so pages 90–91 give you plenty of ideas for use on 'get well soon' cards and gifts.

Stags and bridegrooms are the subject of pages 94–95, with marriage motifs a plenty, but if you want an invite to the wedding, just be careful that the 'old ball and chain' doesn't get offended by this symbol!

The chapter closes with icons associated with retirement, from the customary carriage clock, cardi and cosy slippers, to a Caribbean cruise, tropical sunset and hammock – time to take it easy ...

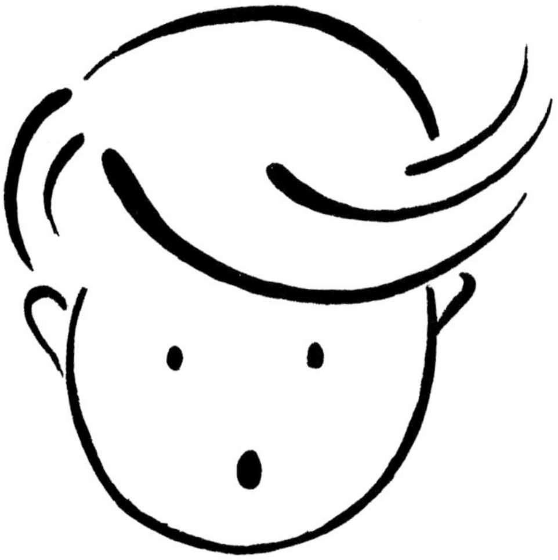

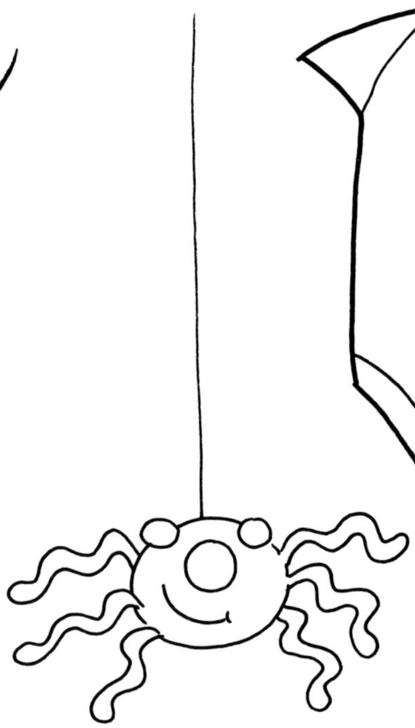

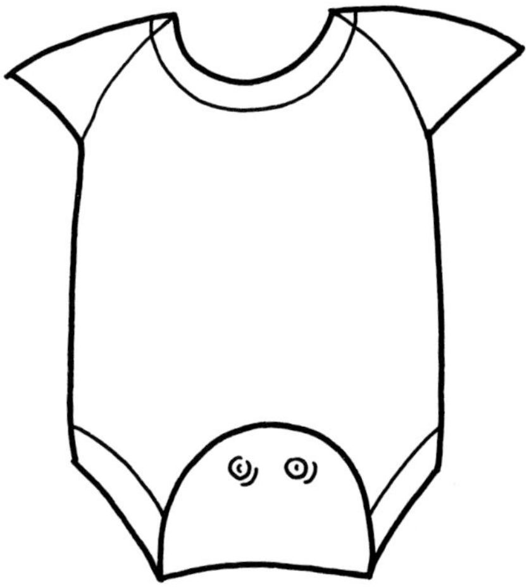

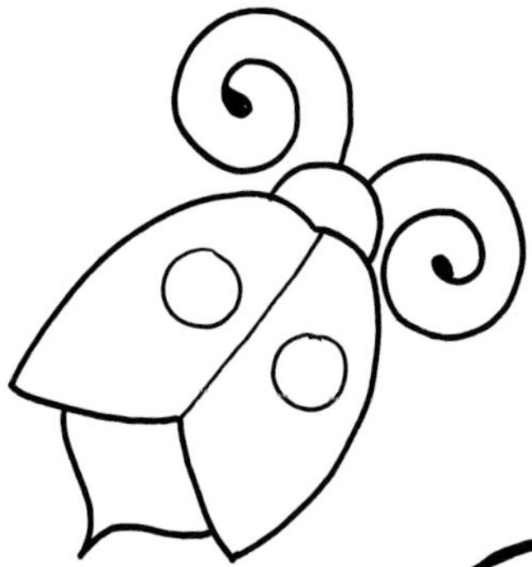

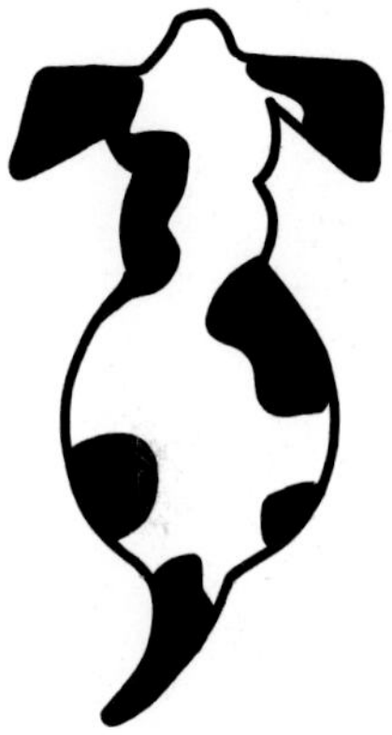

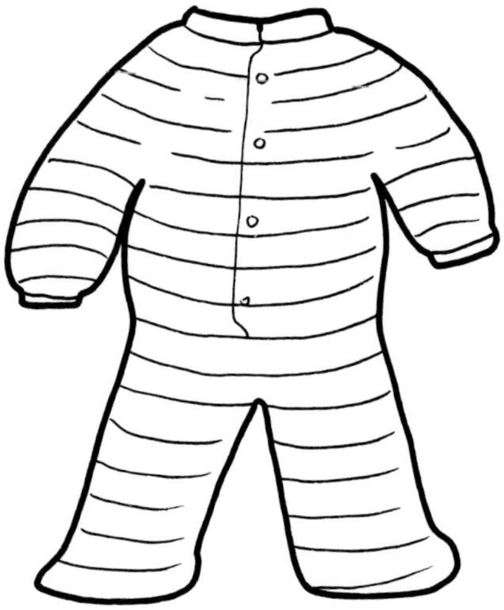

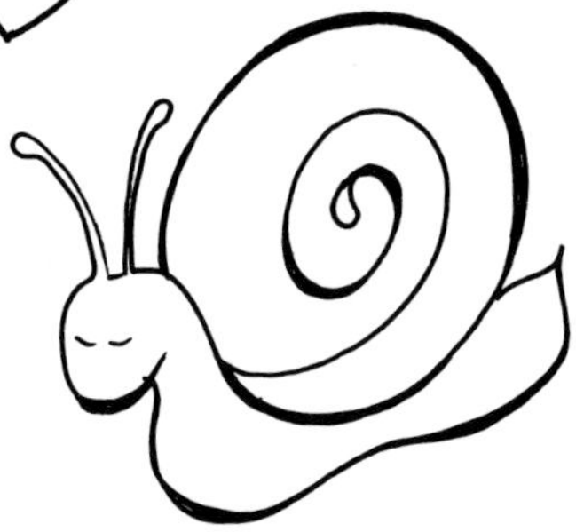

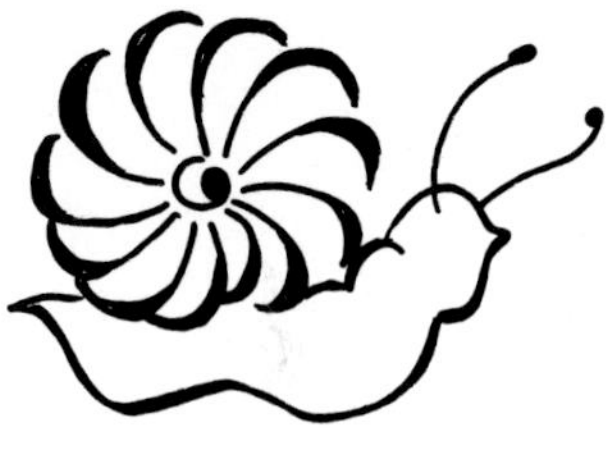

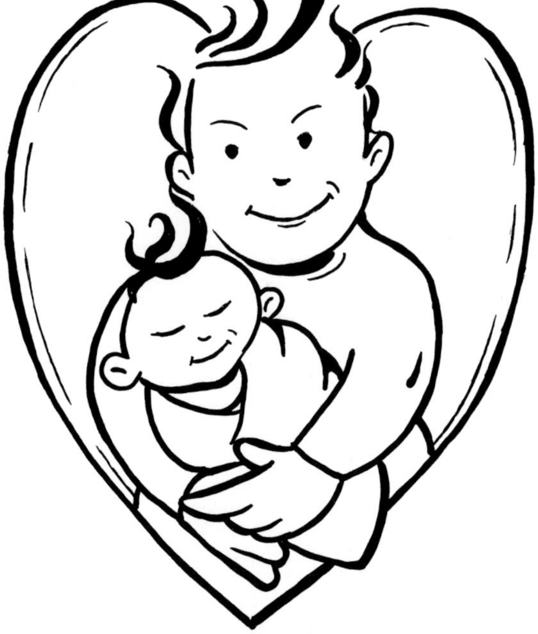

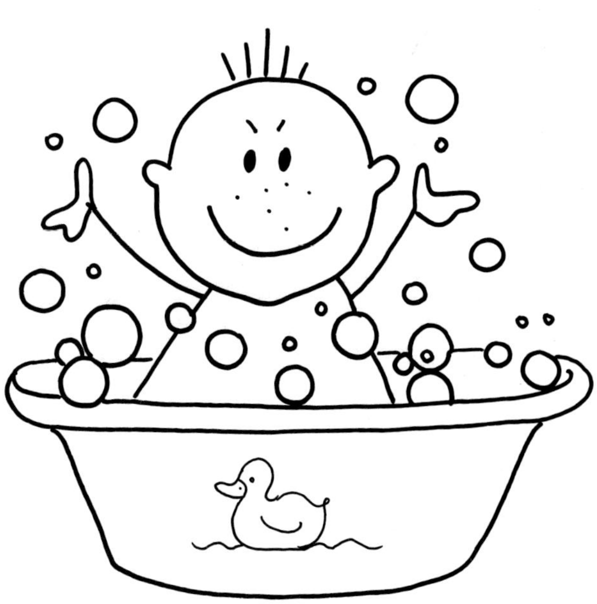

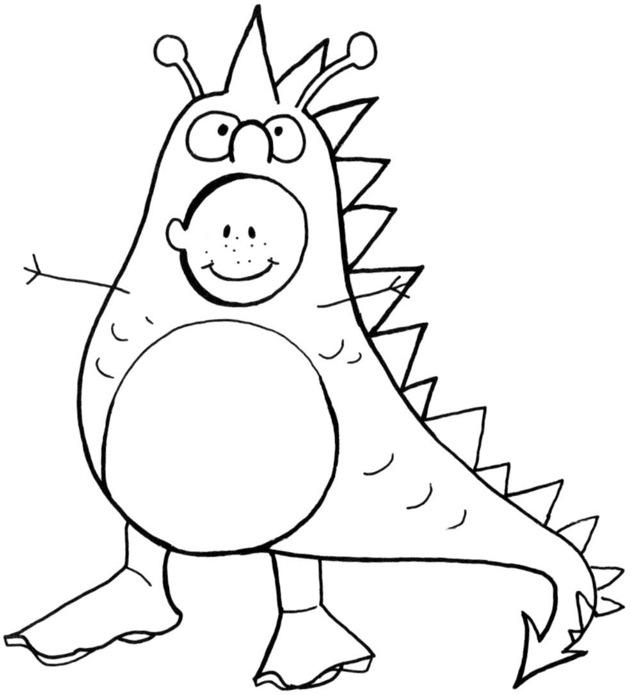

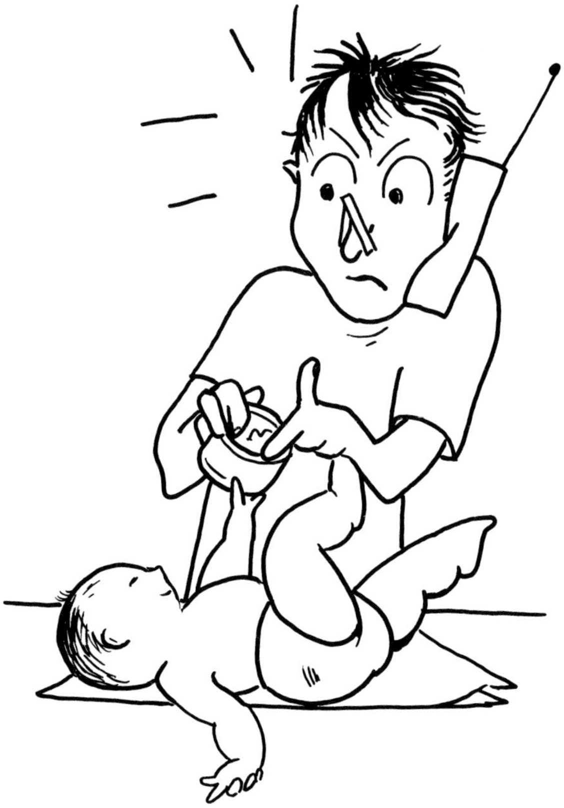

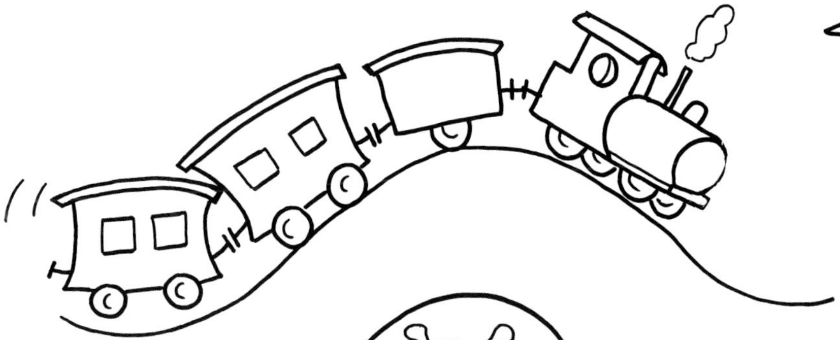

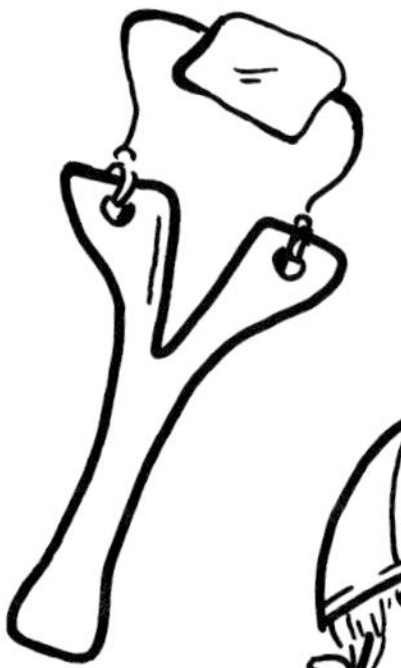

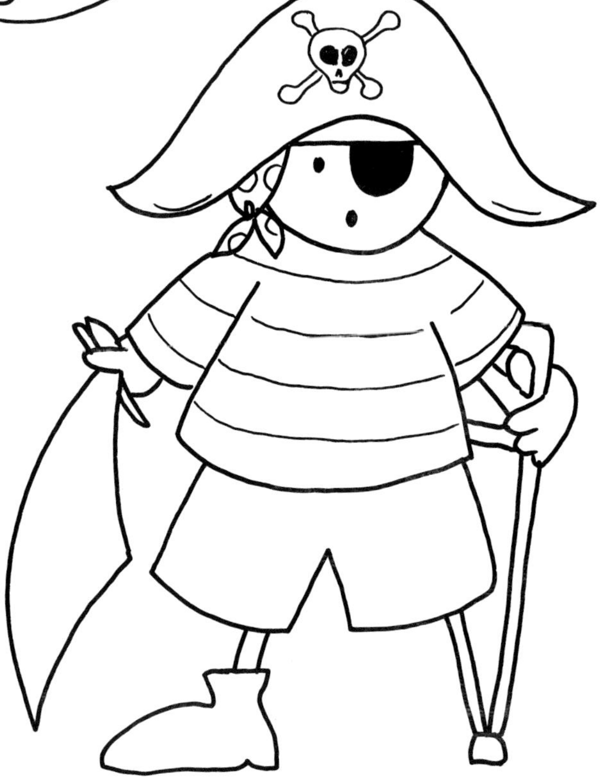

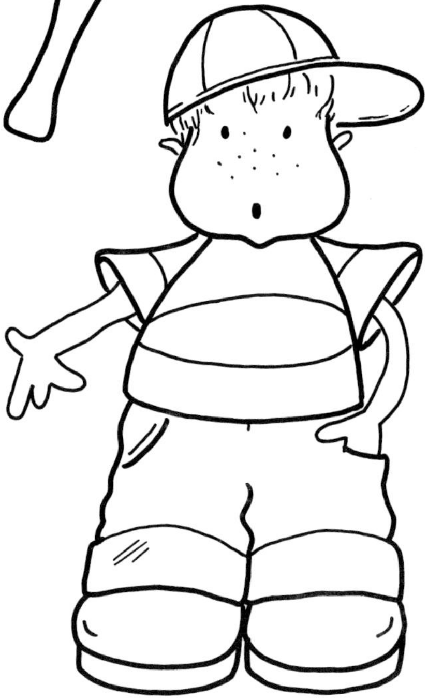

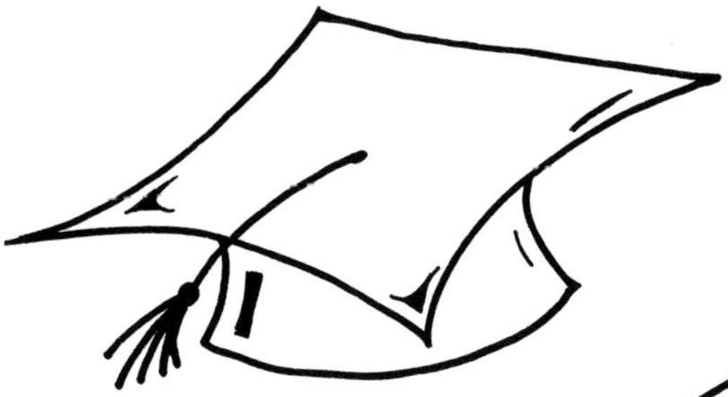

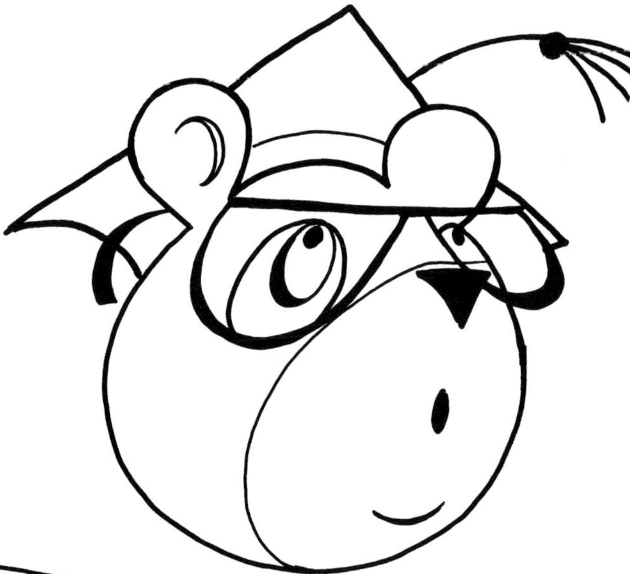

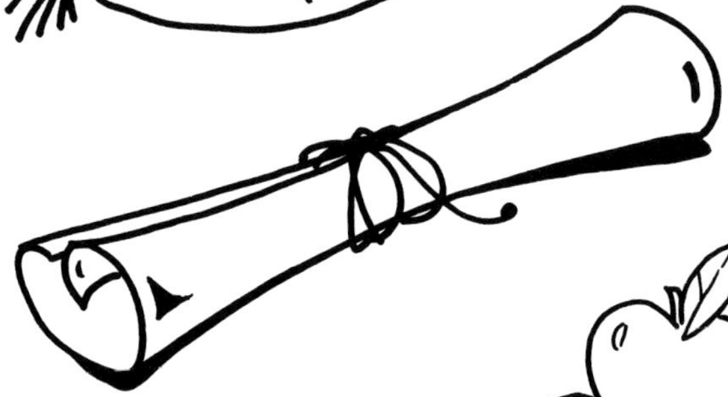

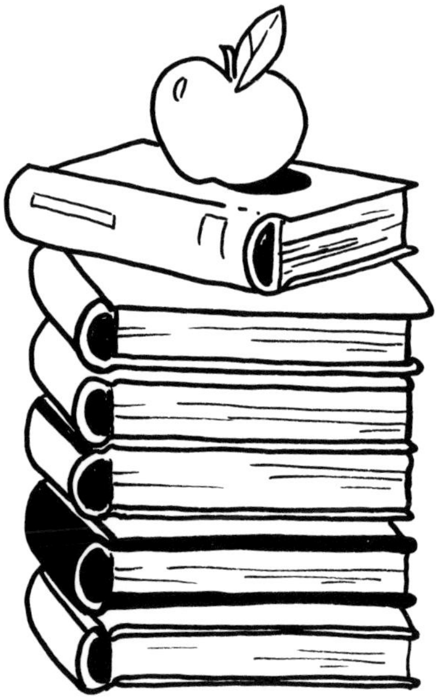

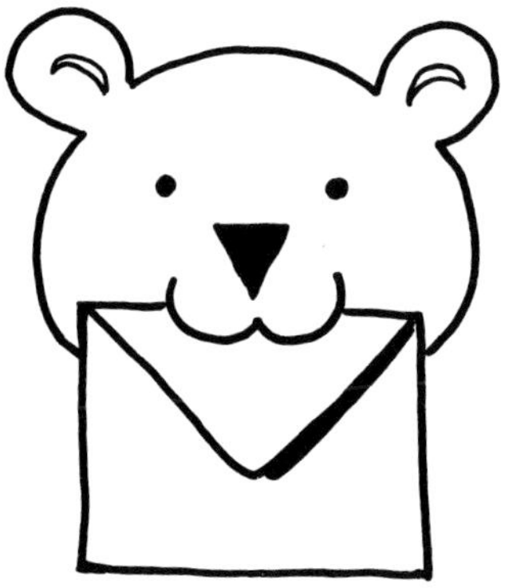

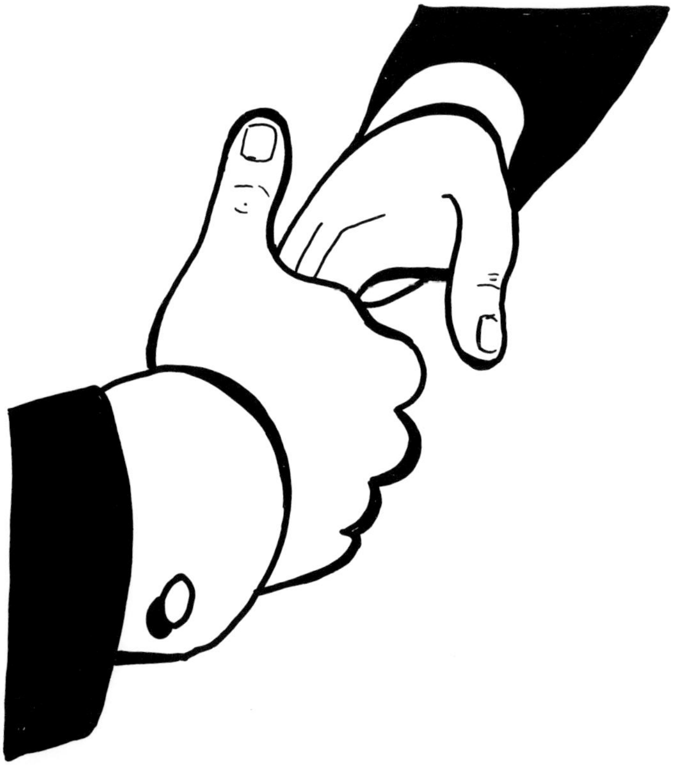

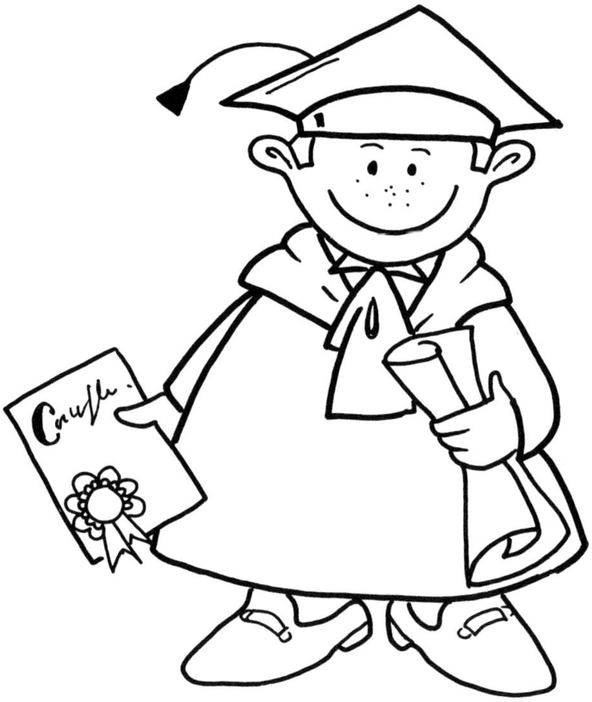

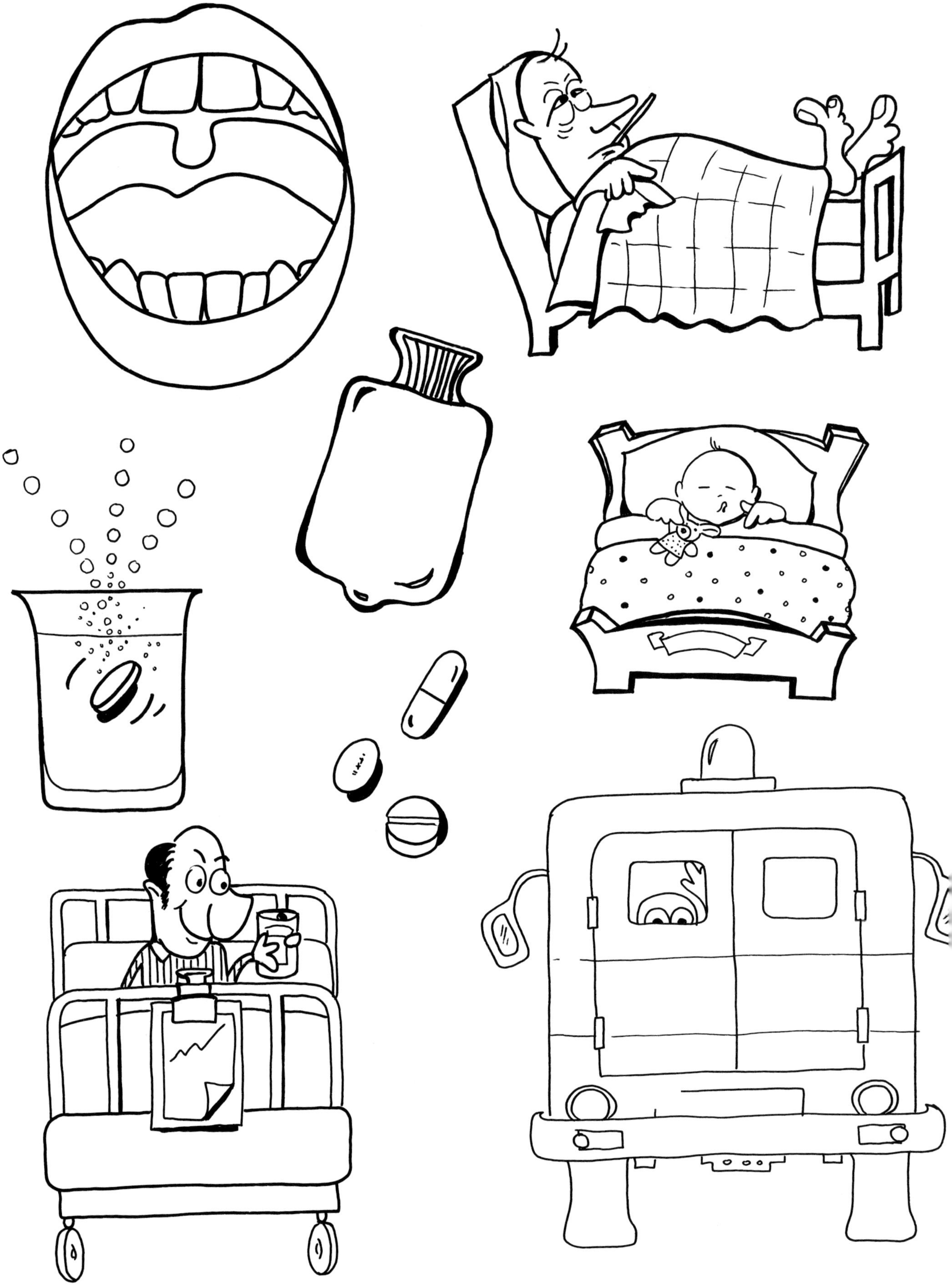

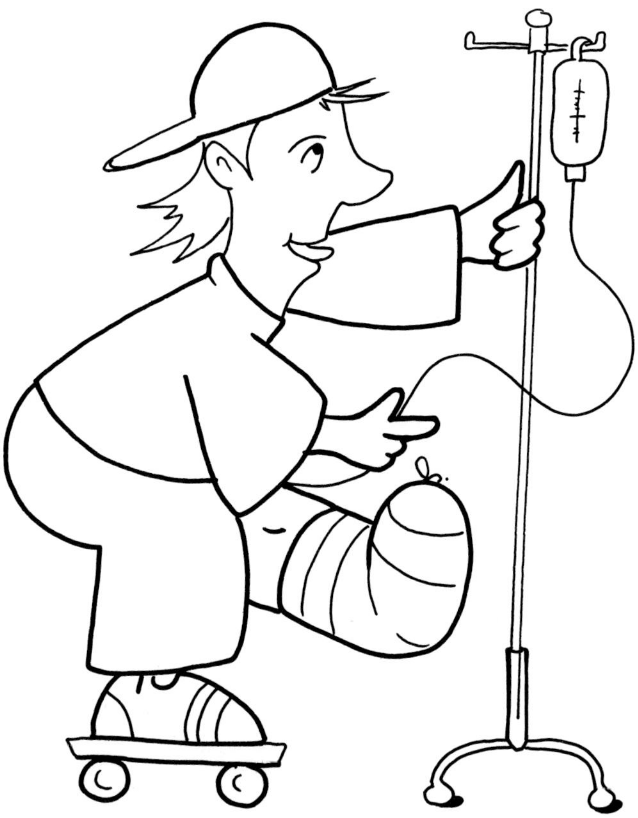

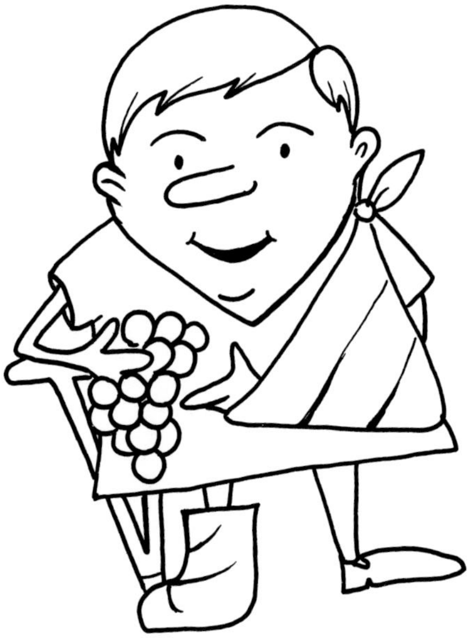

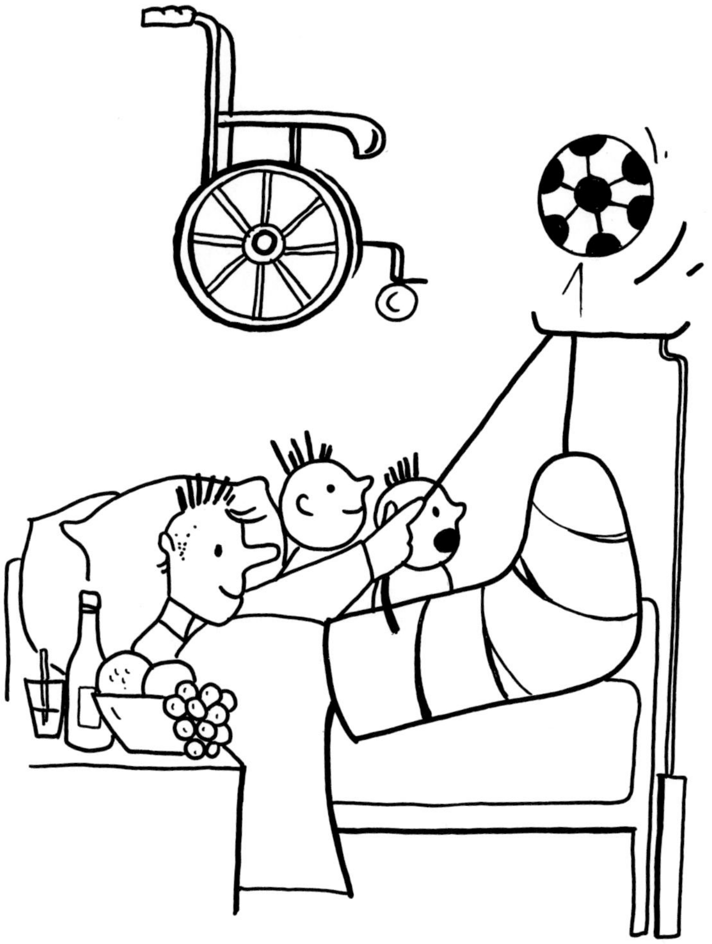

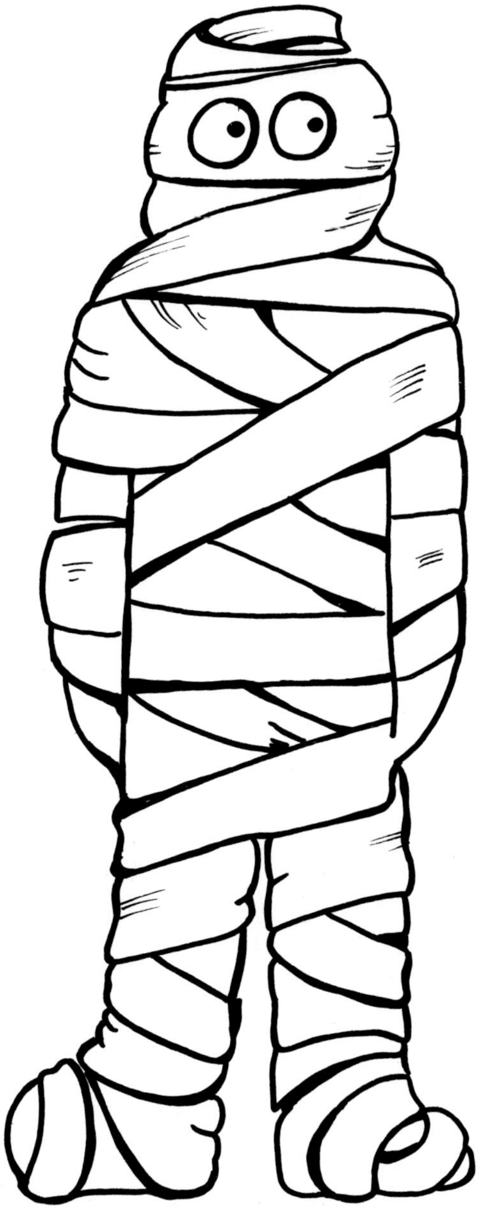

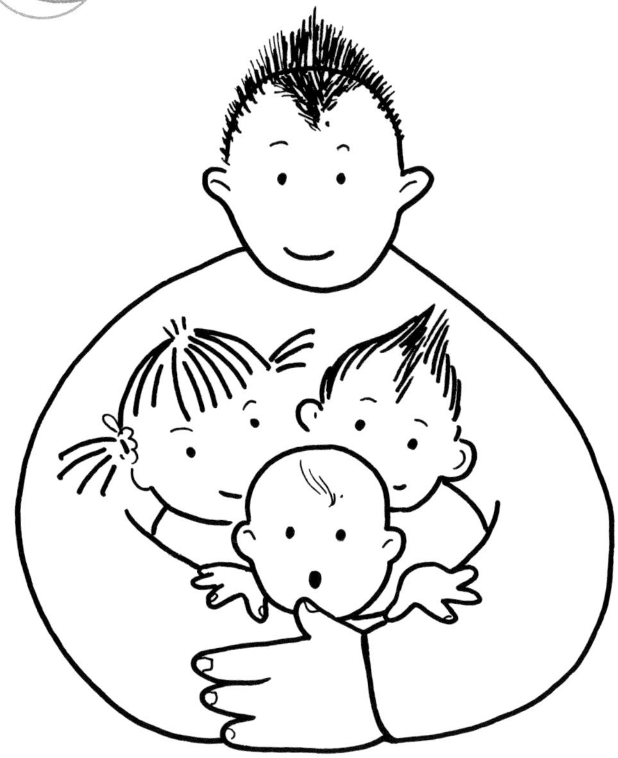

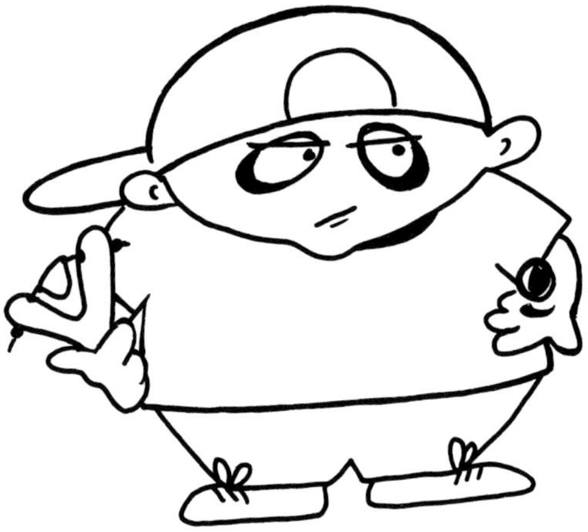

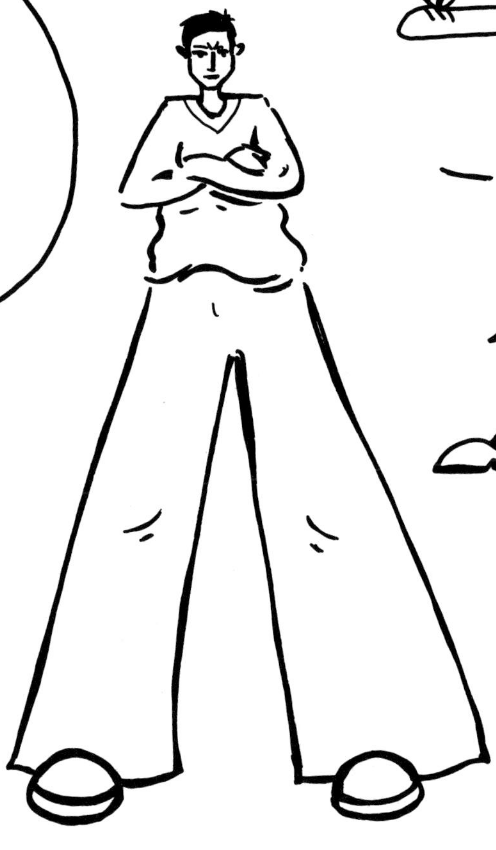

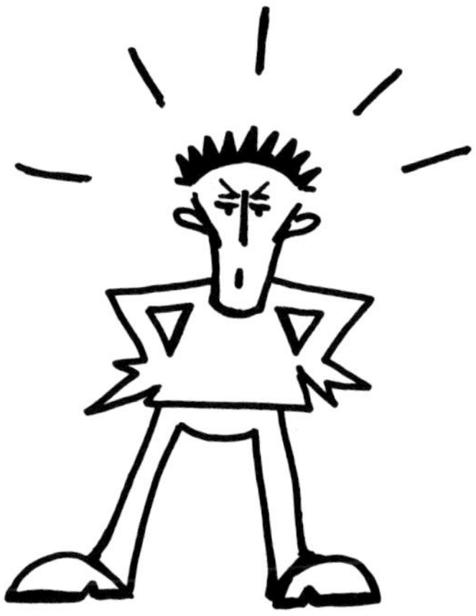

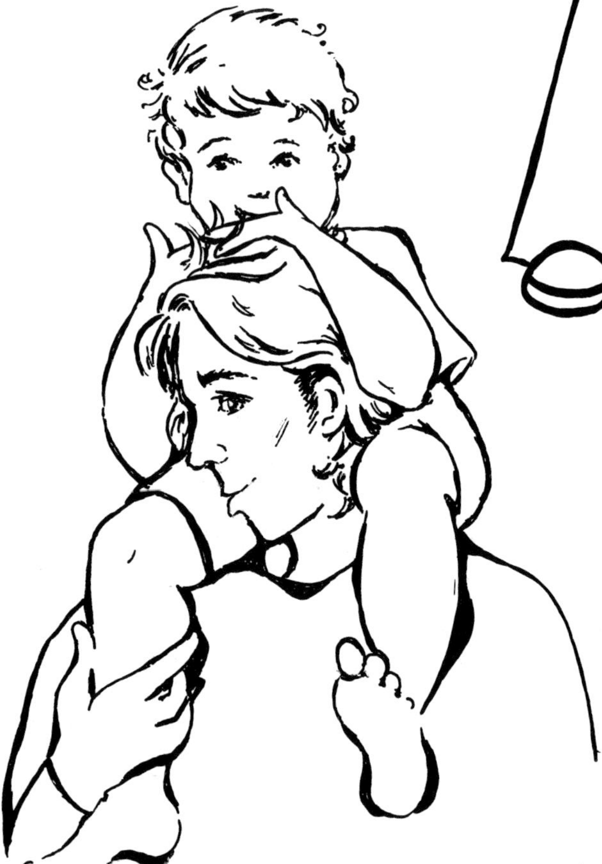

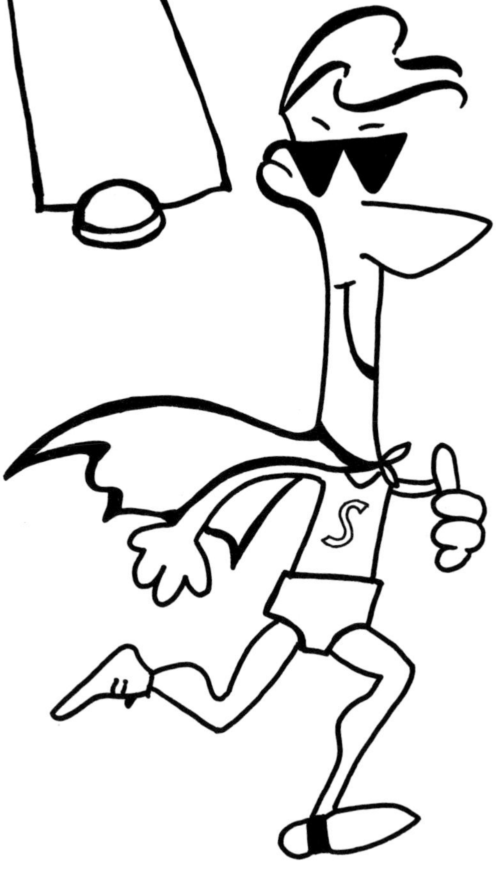

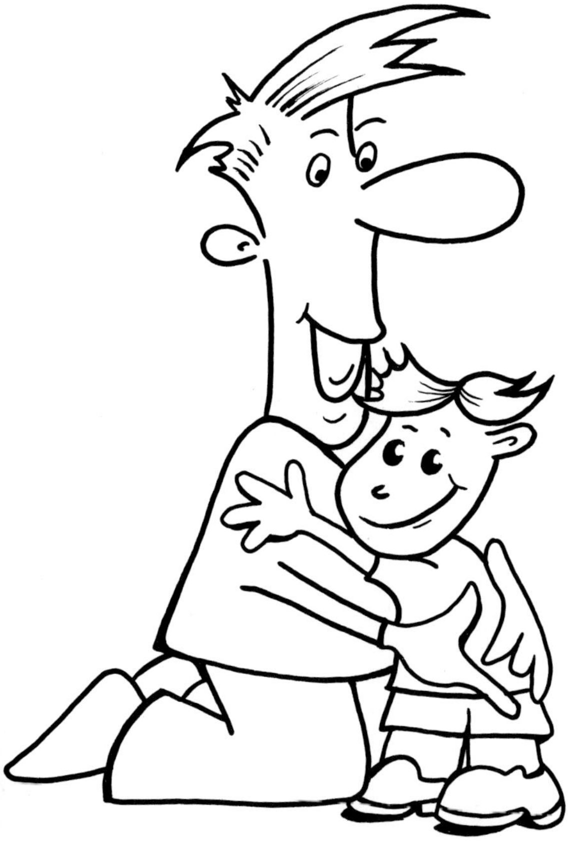

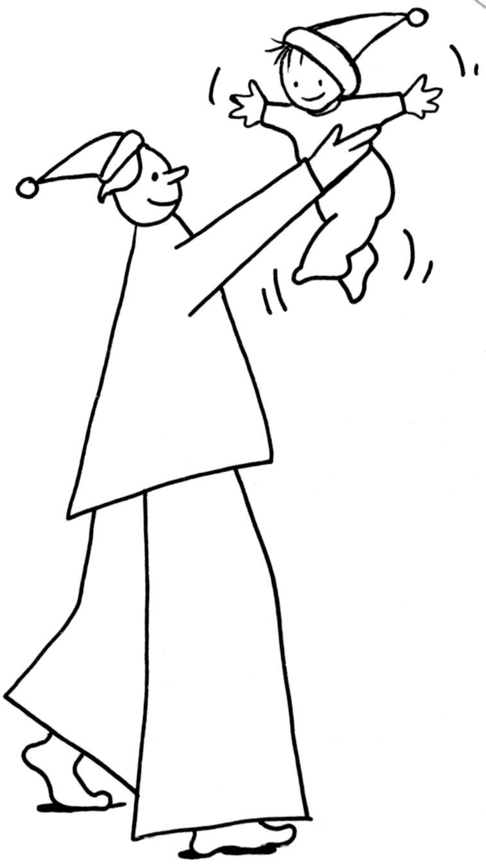

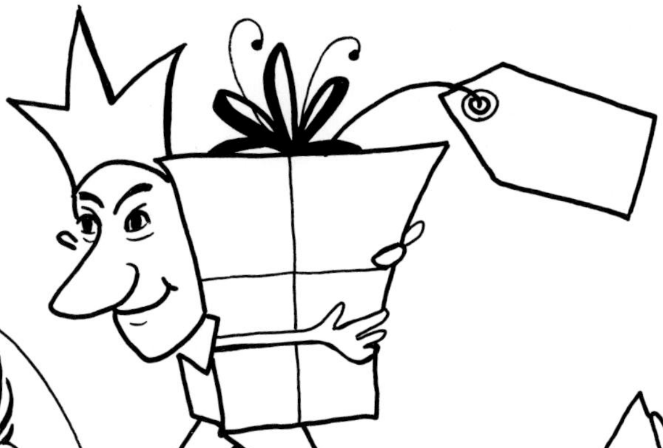

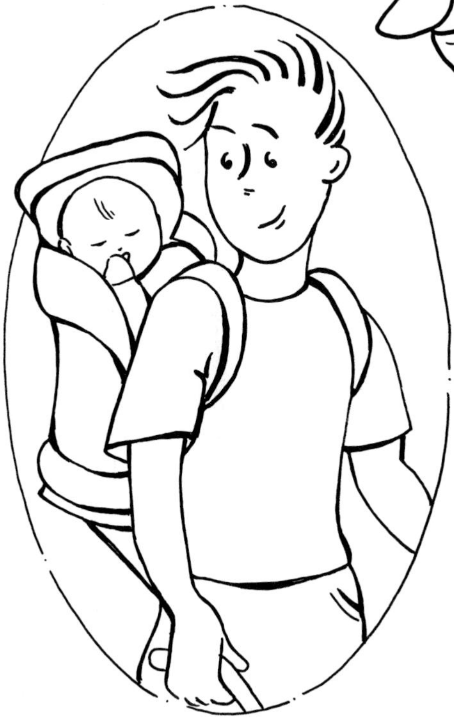

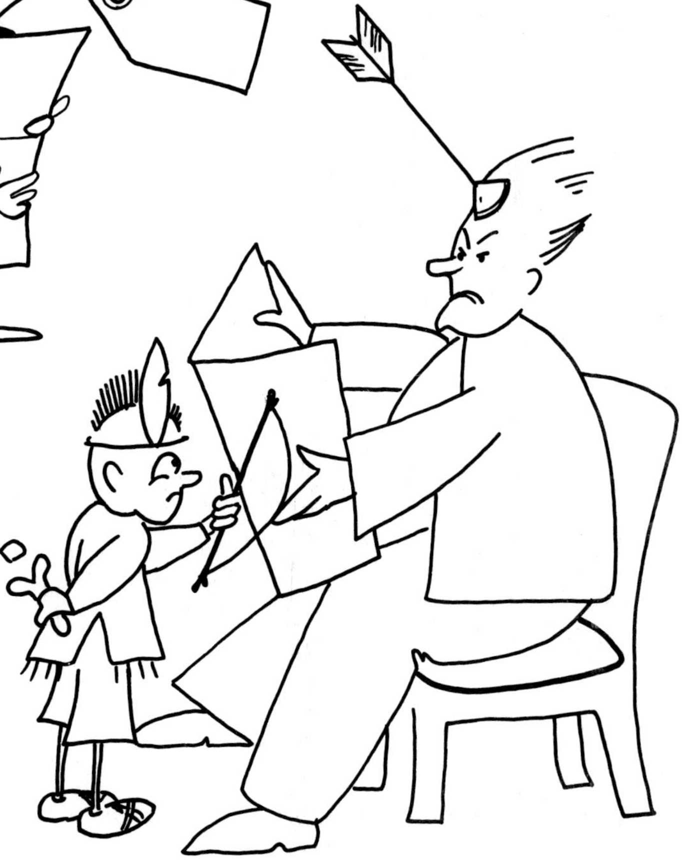

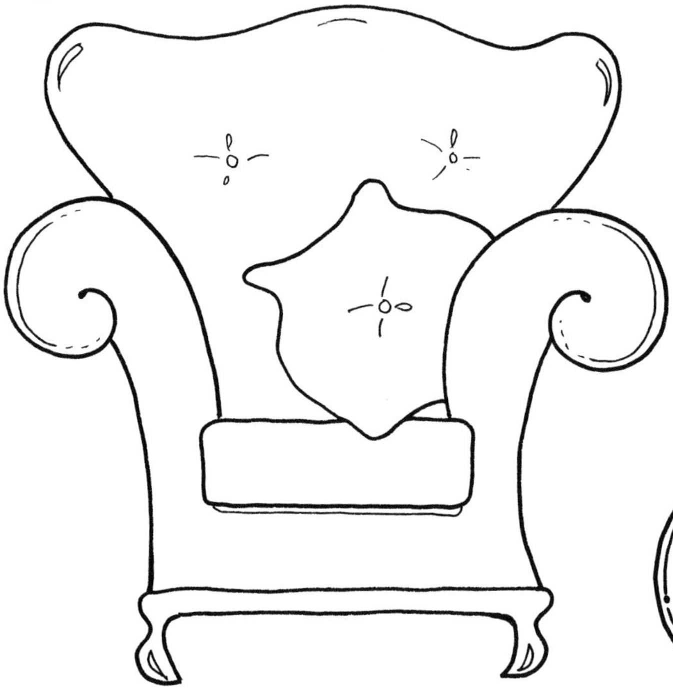

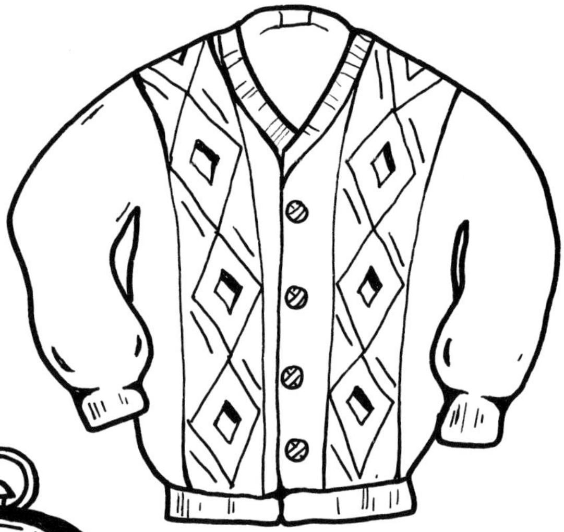

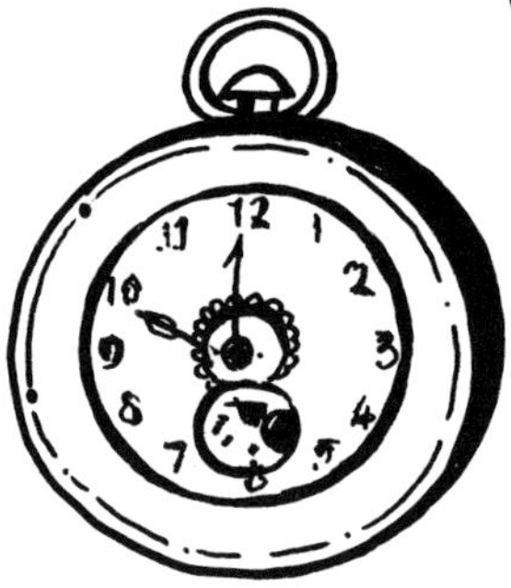

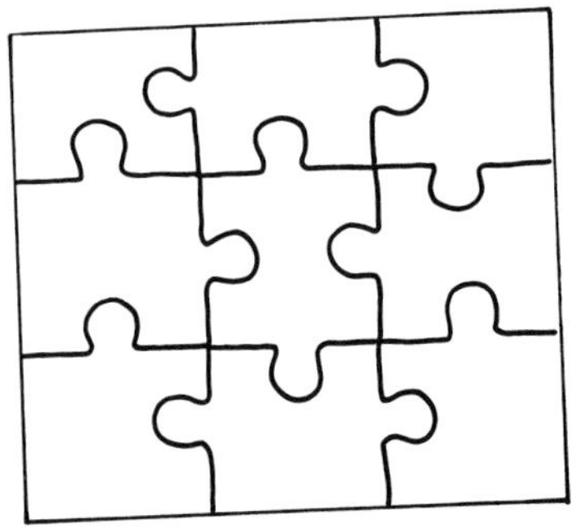

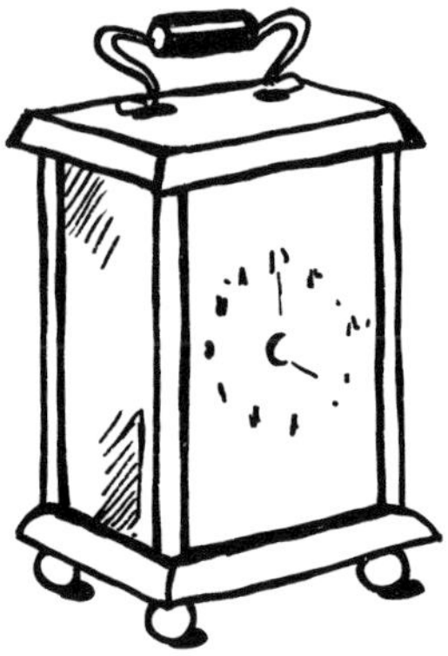

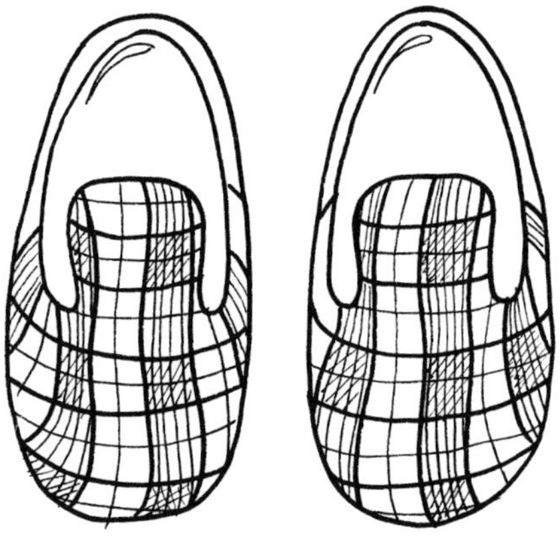

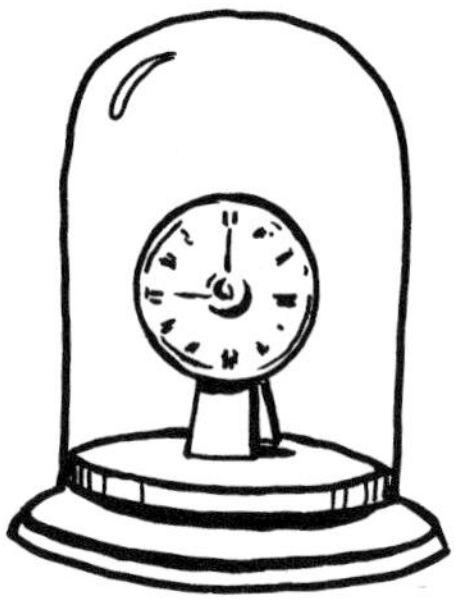

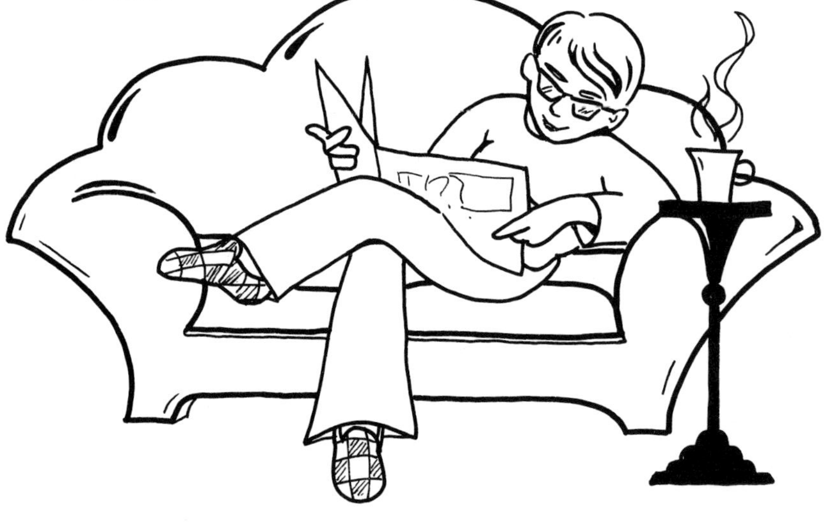

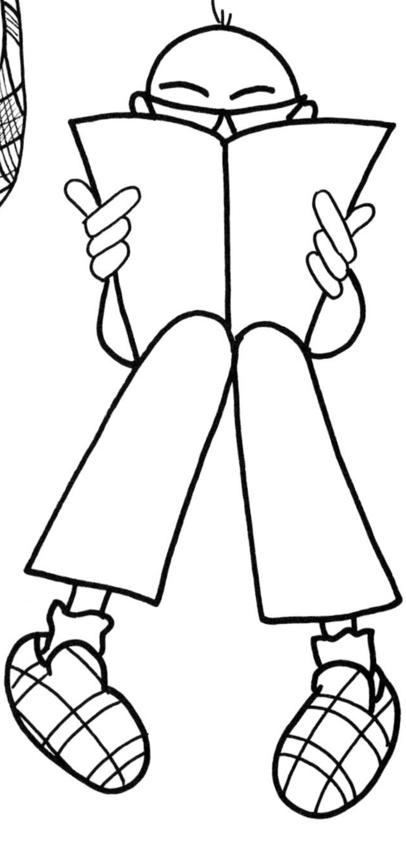

Hobbies

Every man needs a hobby to help him unwind from the stresses of life, and this chapter will give you all the designs you need to show these to the full.

Whether it's a walk in the park (or to the pub) with his canine pal, or a more ambitious mountain ascent, the motifs opposite are perfect to show his love of the great outdoors.

The fresh air theme continues with designs depicting a gentle round of golf and those more suited to fitness fanatics and adrenaline junkies, including bungee jumping, handgliding, scuba diving and parachuting.

All that exercise is bound to work up an appetite, so get straight to his heart through his stomach with the emblems on pages 104–105, which have been used to make the barbecue card on page 20.

If he's a fan of cards, dice and board games, or even snooker and bowls turn to pages 106–107, while keen gardeners can be kept satisfied by the motifs on pages 108–109.

Fishing, exotic pets, stamp collecting, photography, film, model making and fossil-hunting designs feature on pages 110–111, and fabulous holiday pursuits, from safari tours to theme parks, complete the chapter.

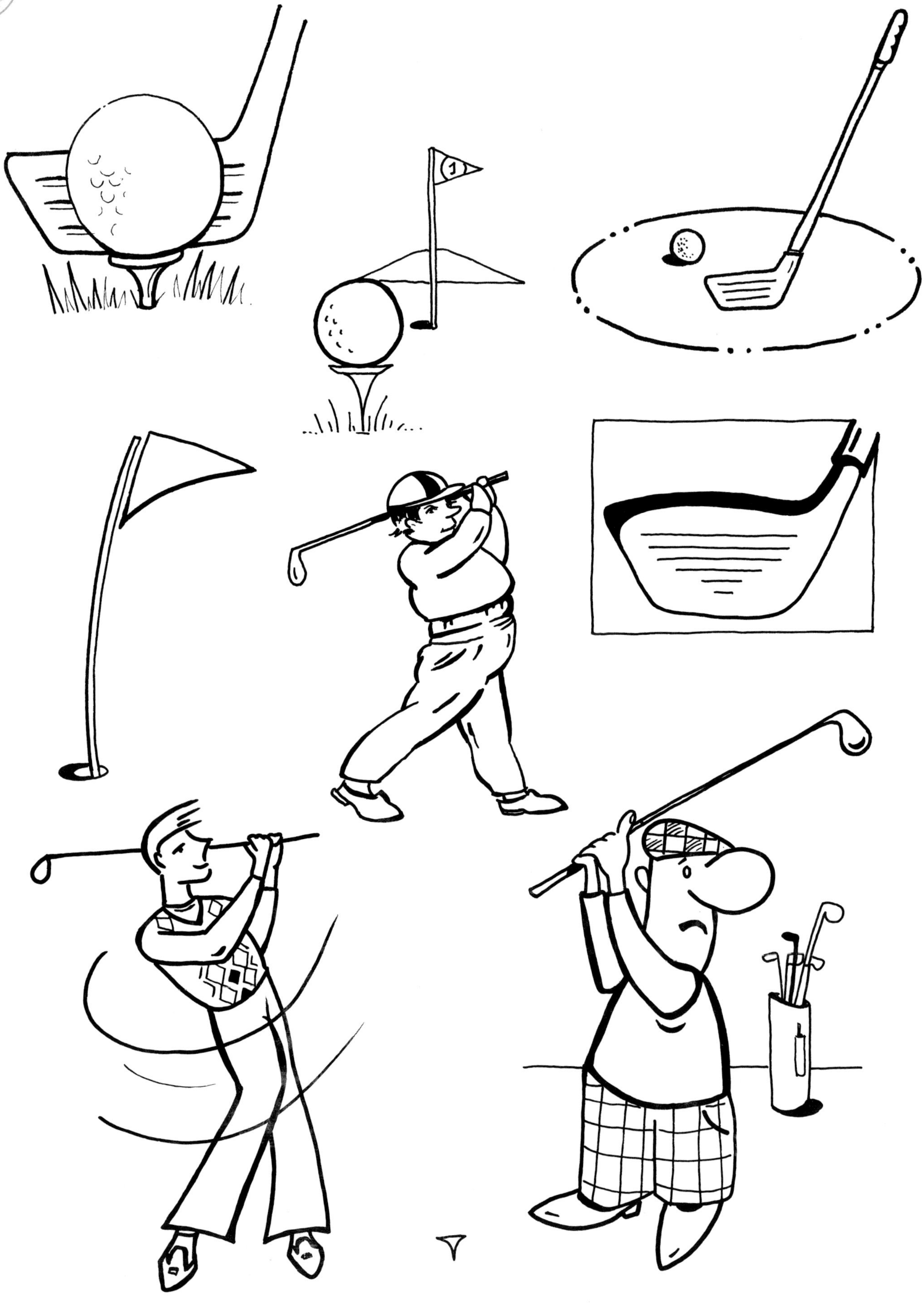

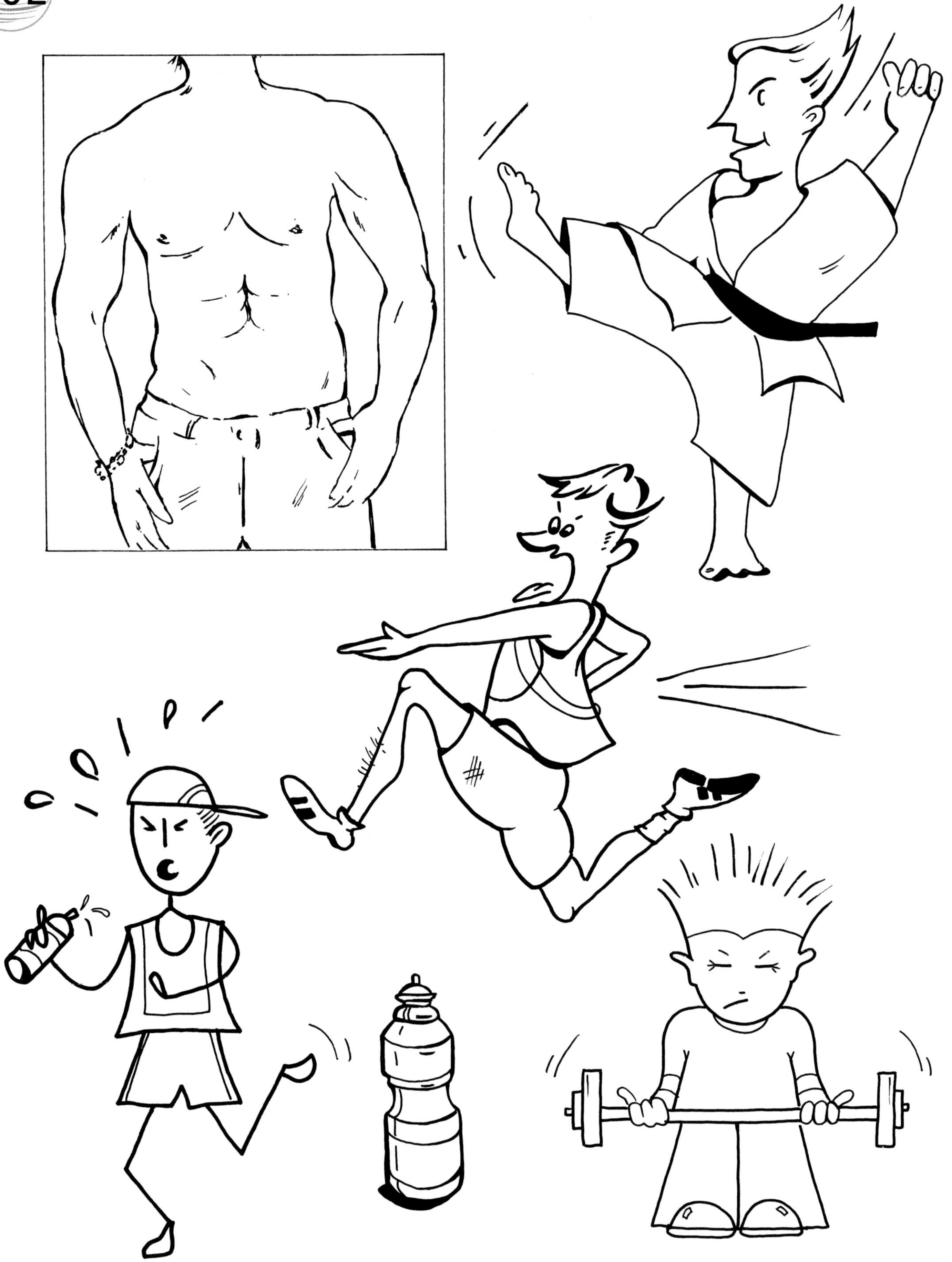

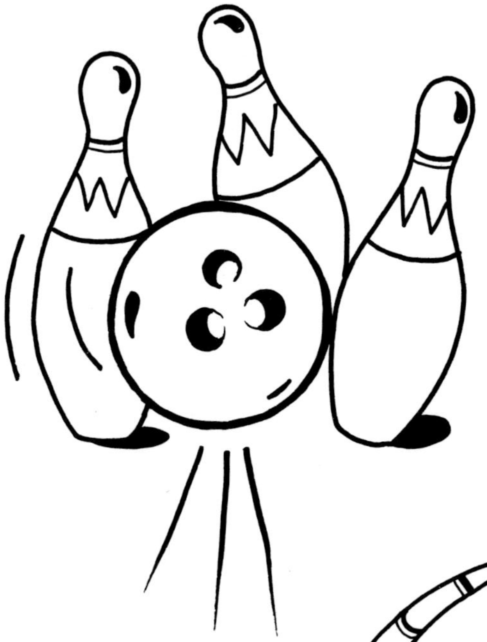

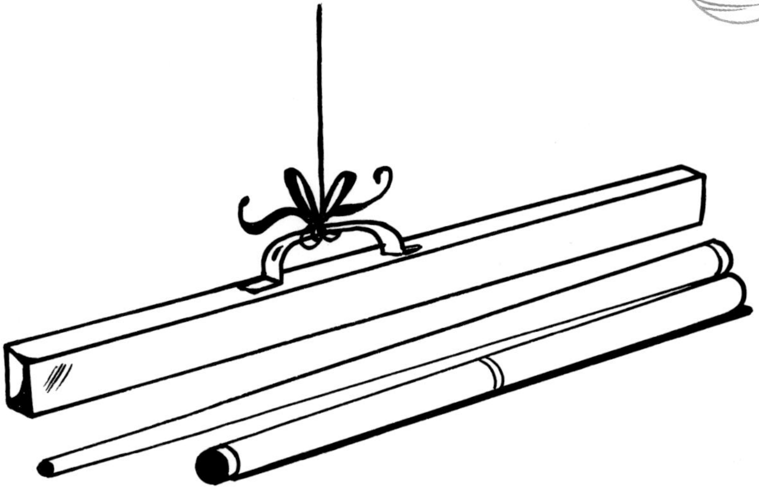

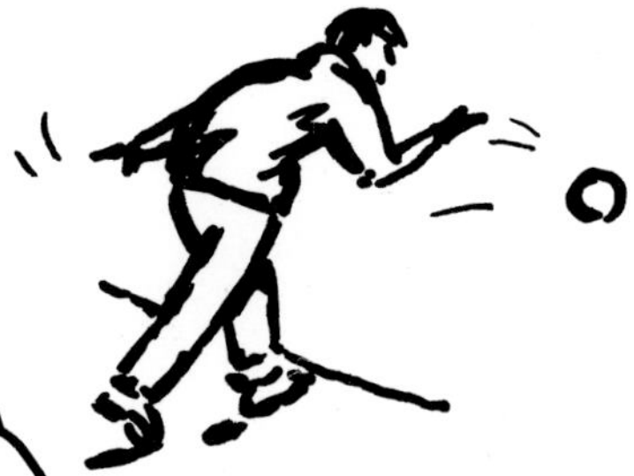

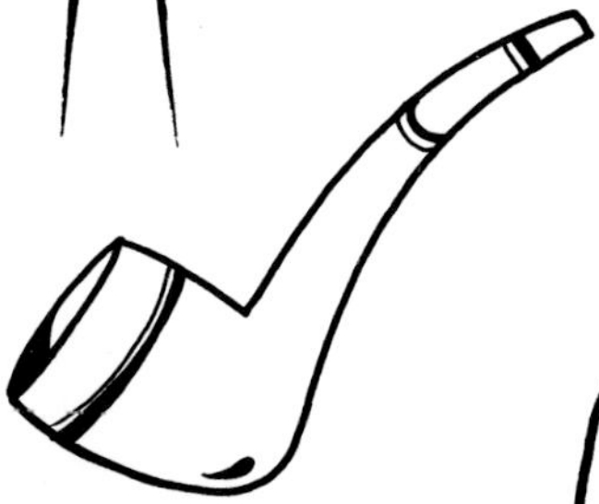

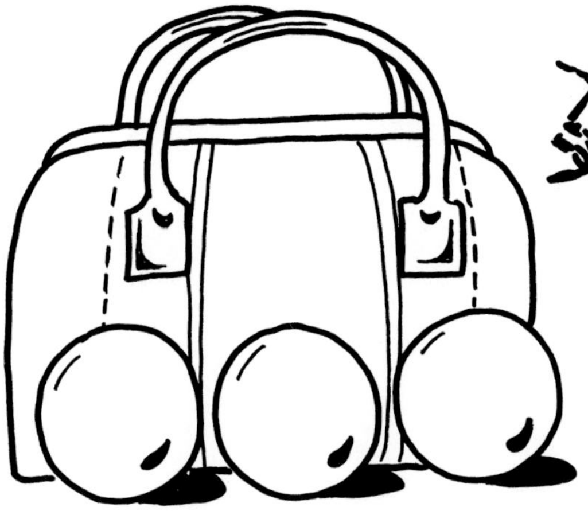

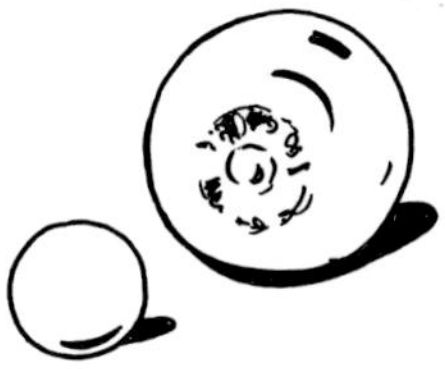

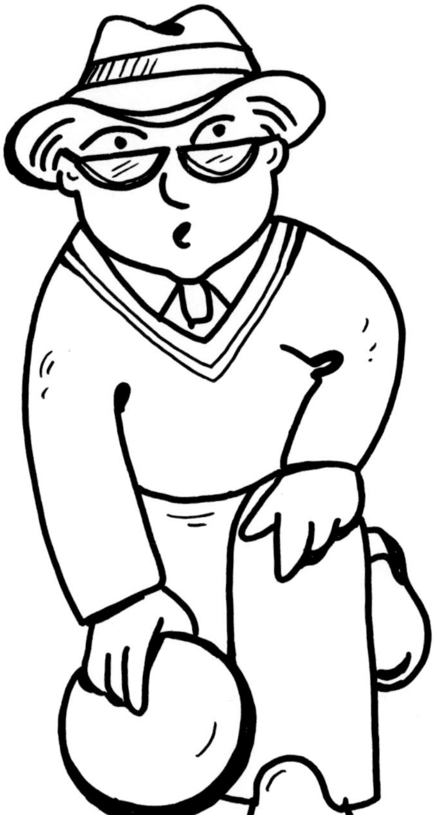

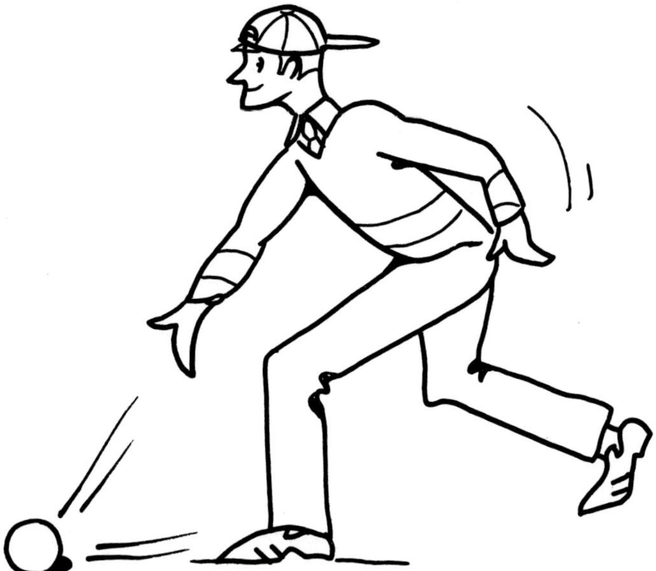

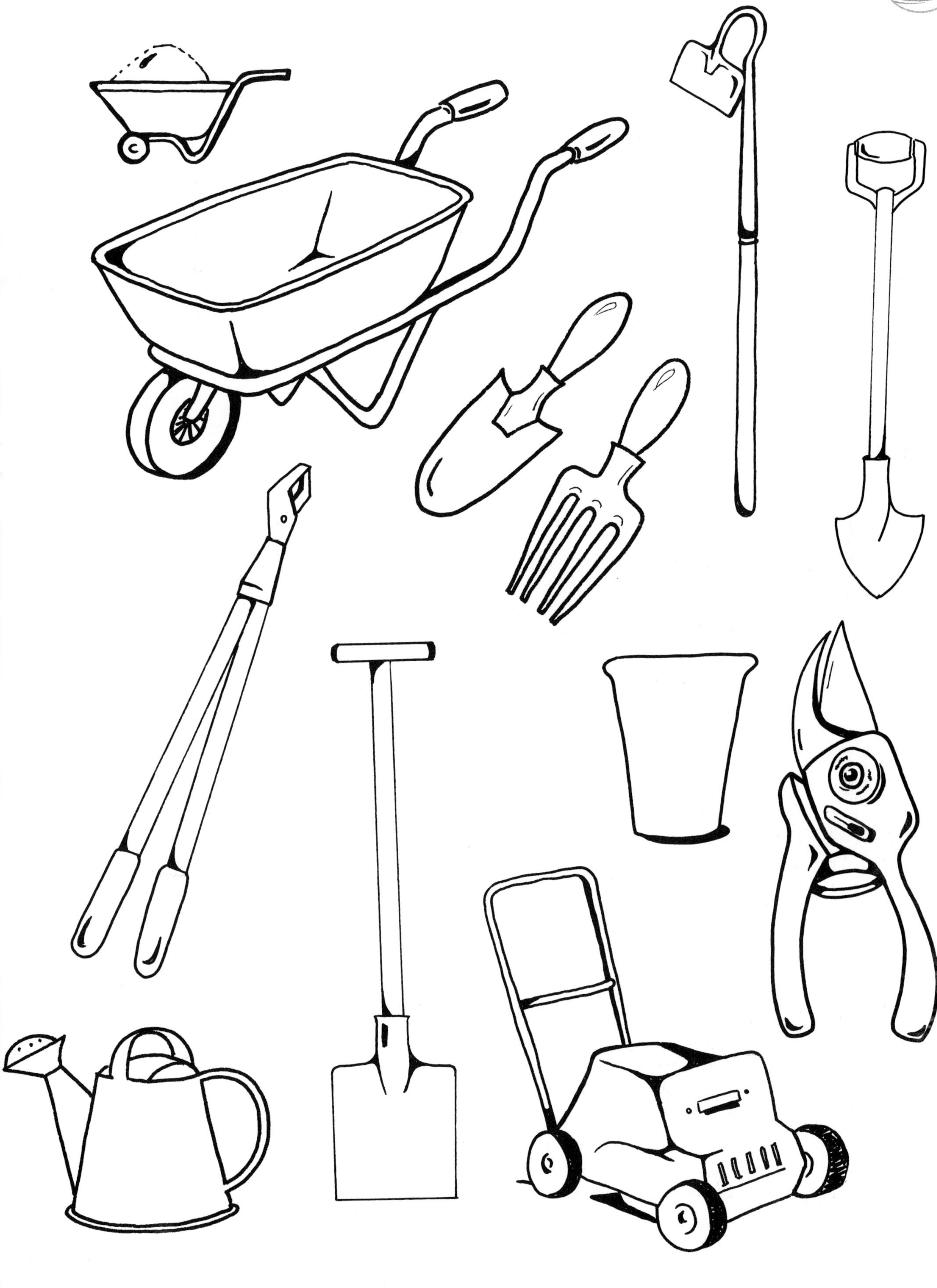

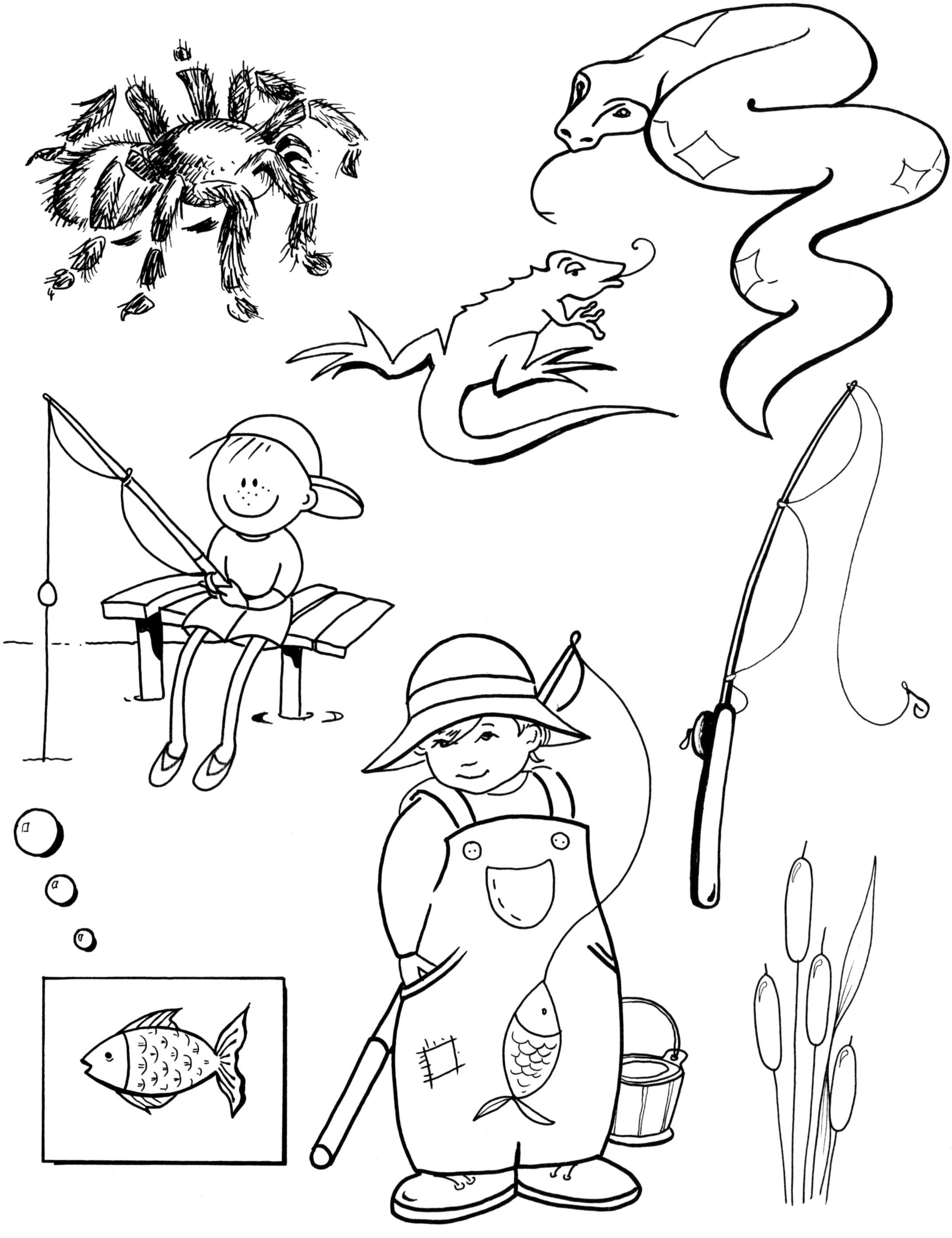

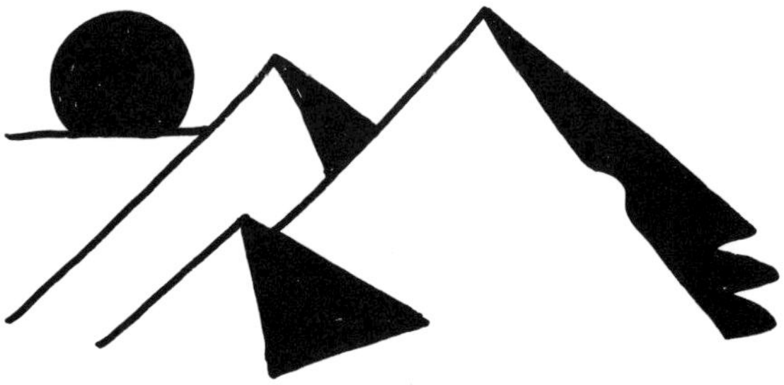

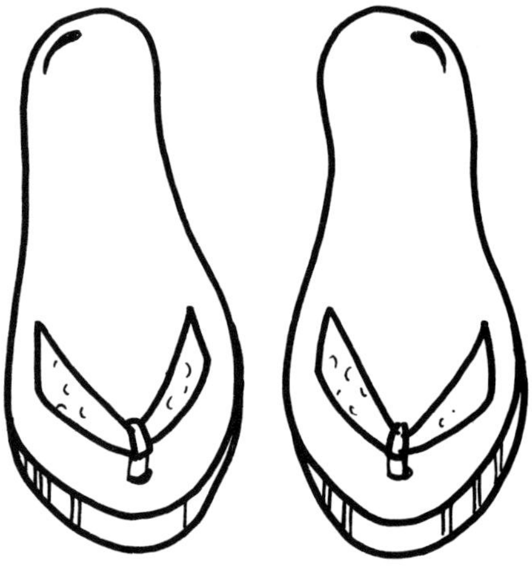

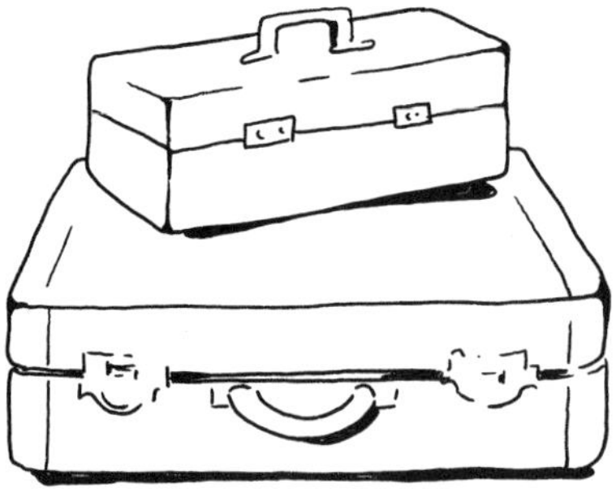

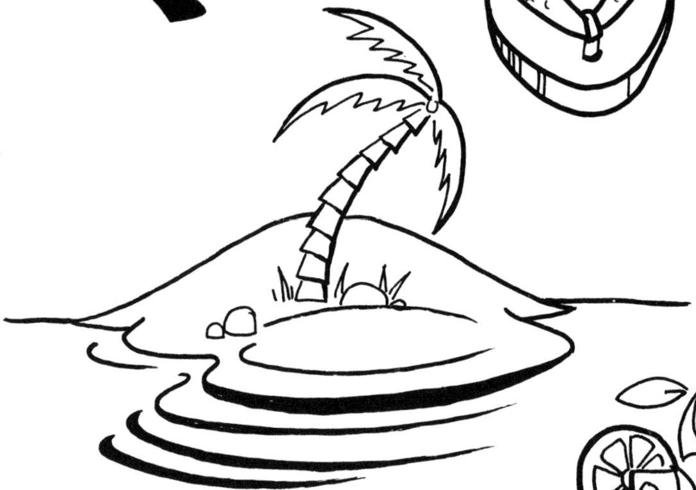

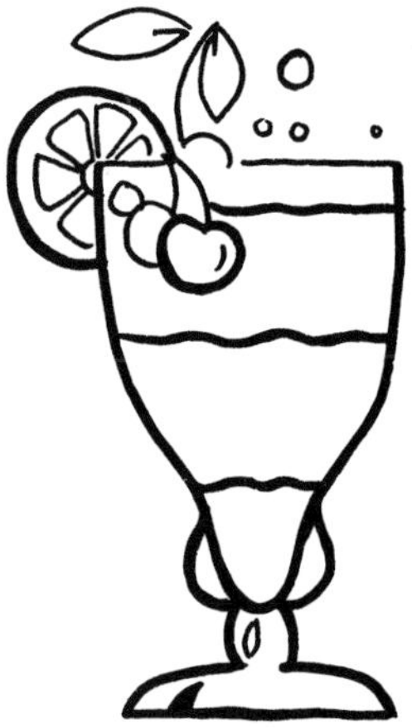

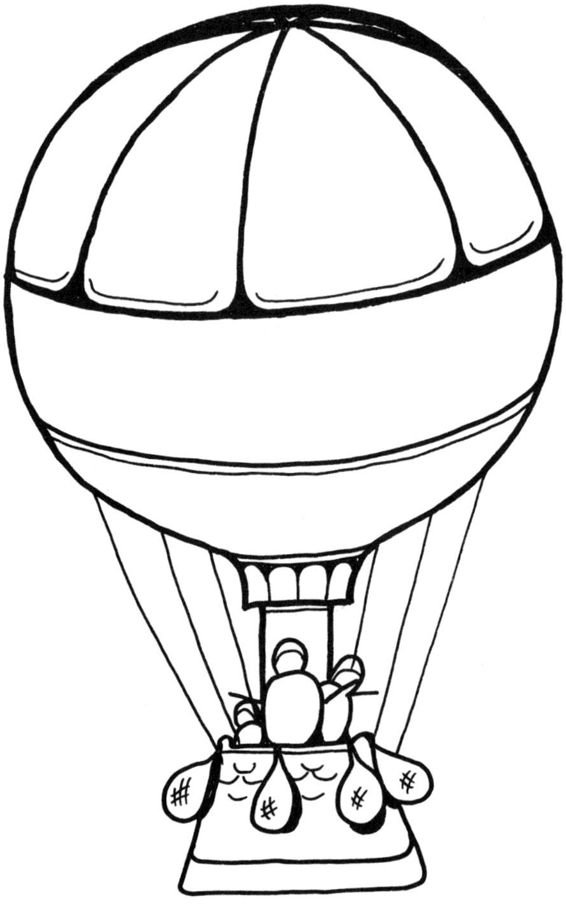

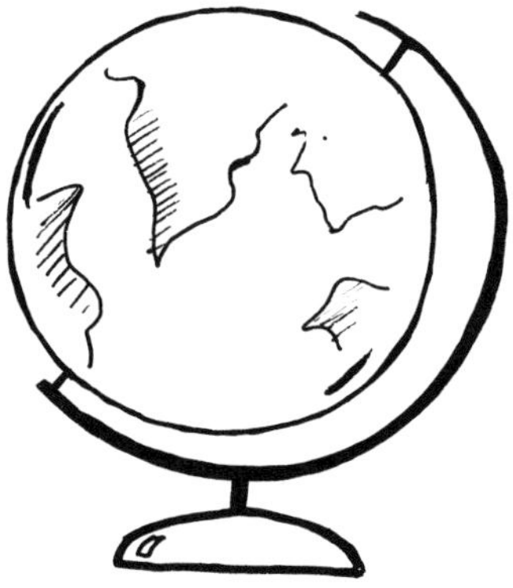

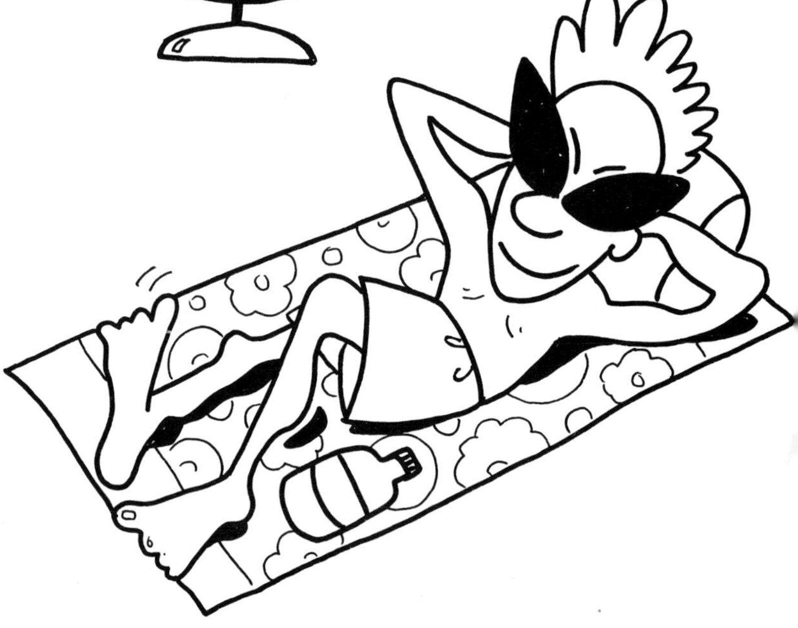

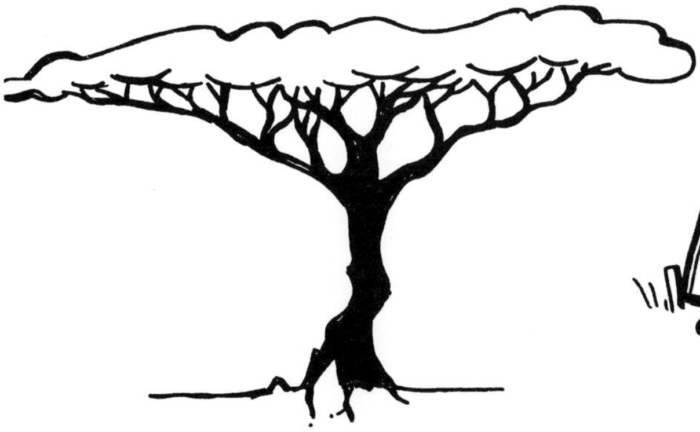

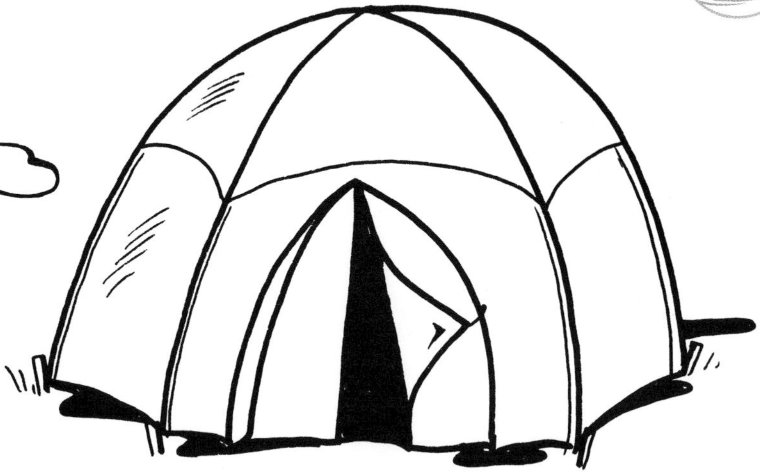

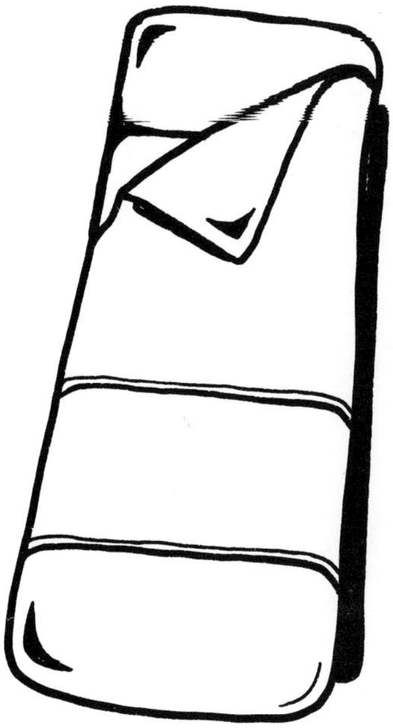

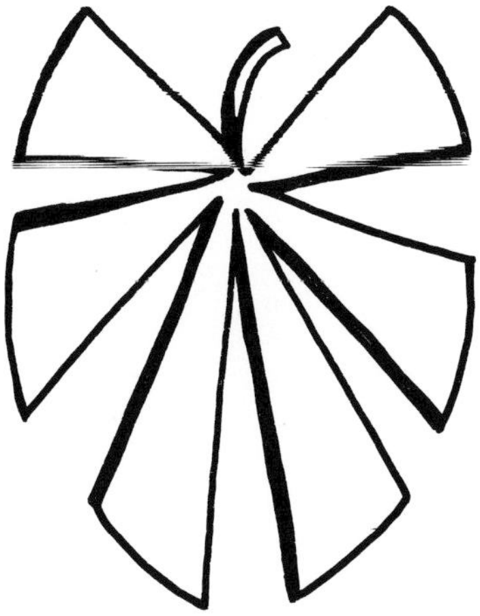

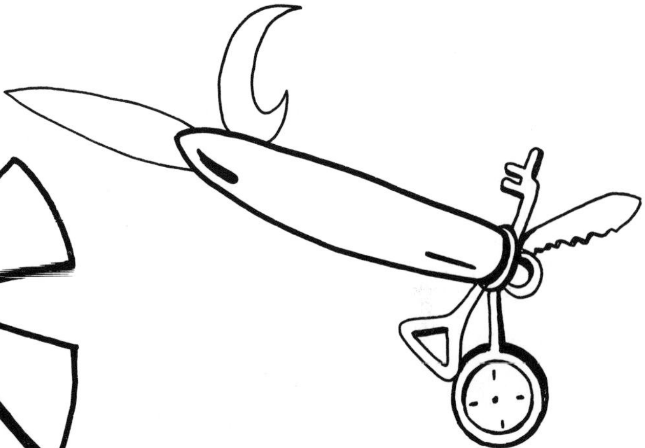

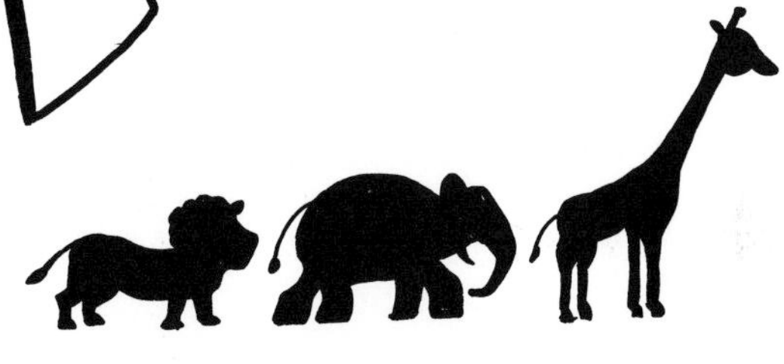

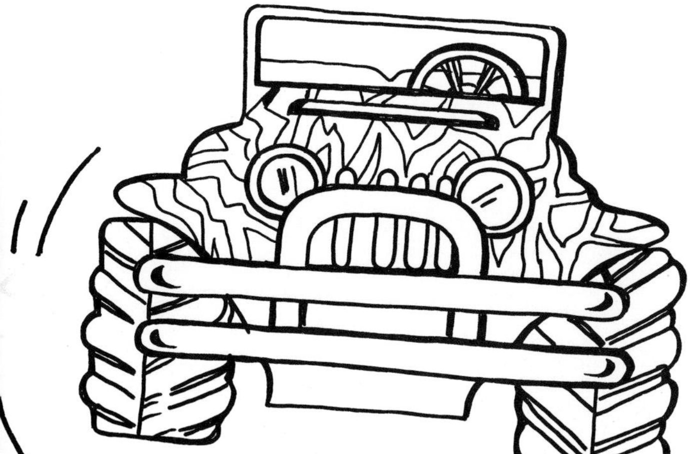

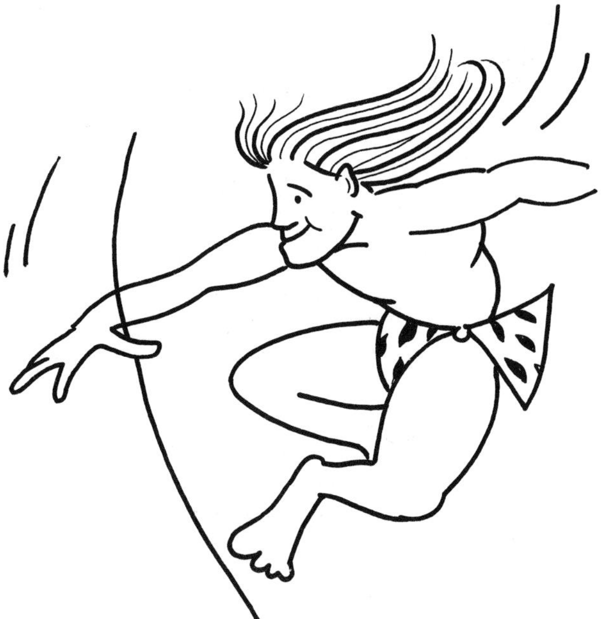

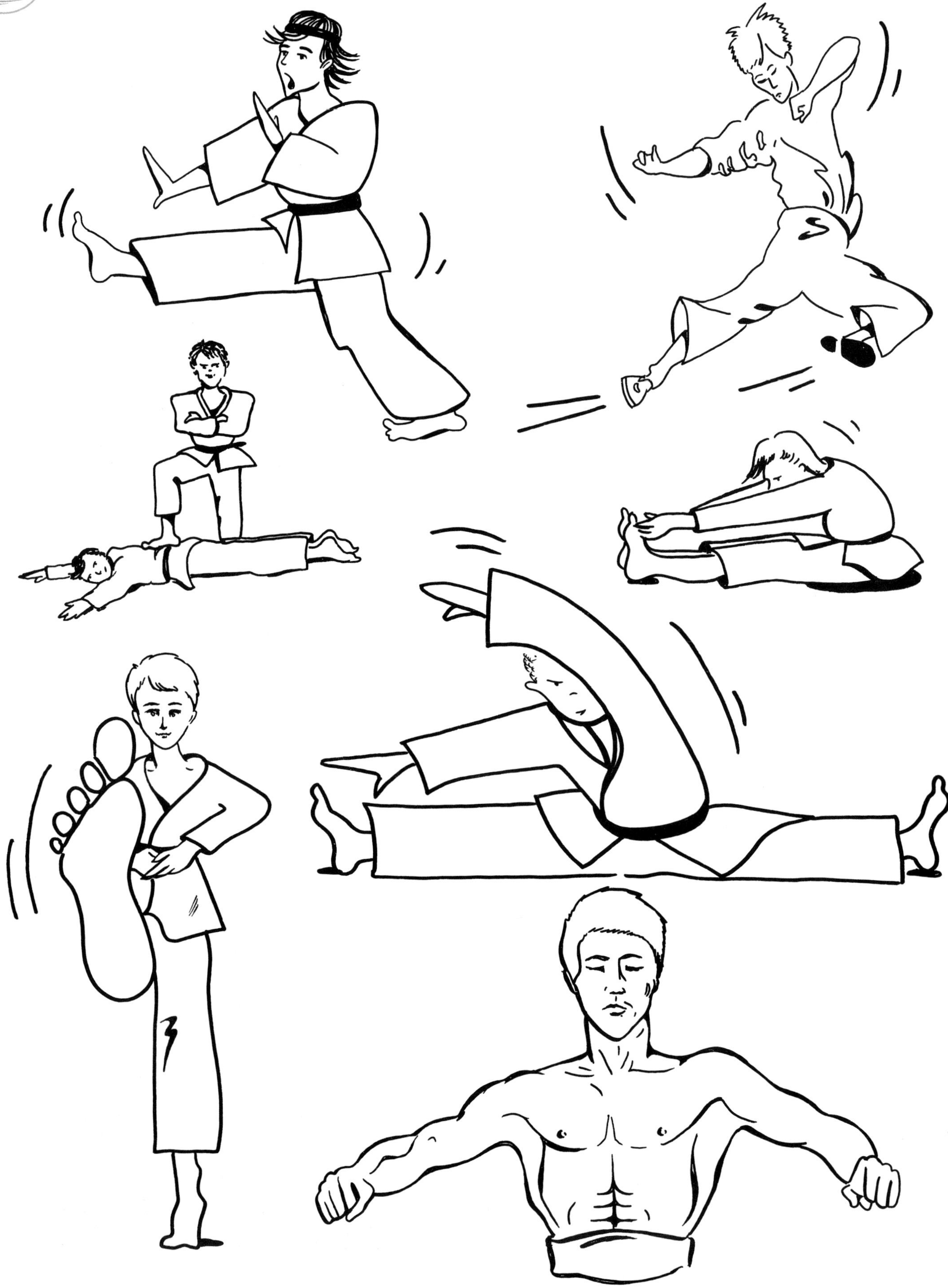

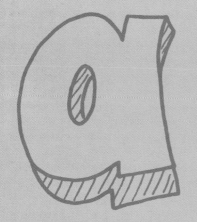

Finishing touches

Borders and frames can help give your designs a final bit of polish, while banners and emblems give you the opportunity to add your own message to personalize your creations.

The ideas given here are fairly limited, but they can be adapted to give you numerous different options. Use them as a springboard for your own ideas too, allowing yourself the creativity to create your own border effects.

The alphabets are also just a starting point – there are an endless variety of typefaces and fonts that can be used to embellish your projects. Try these ideas for starters, but let your imagination run riot when it comes to lettering, and you will be sure to create some truly inspirational designs.

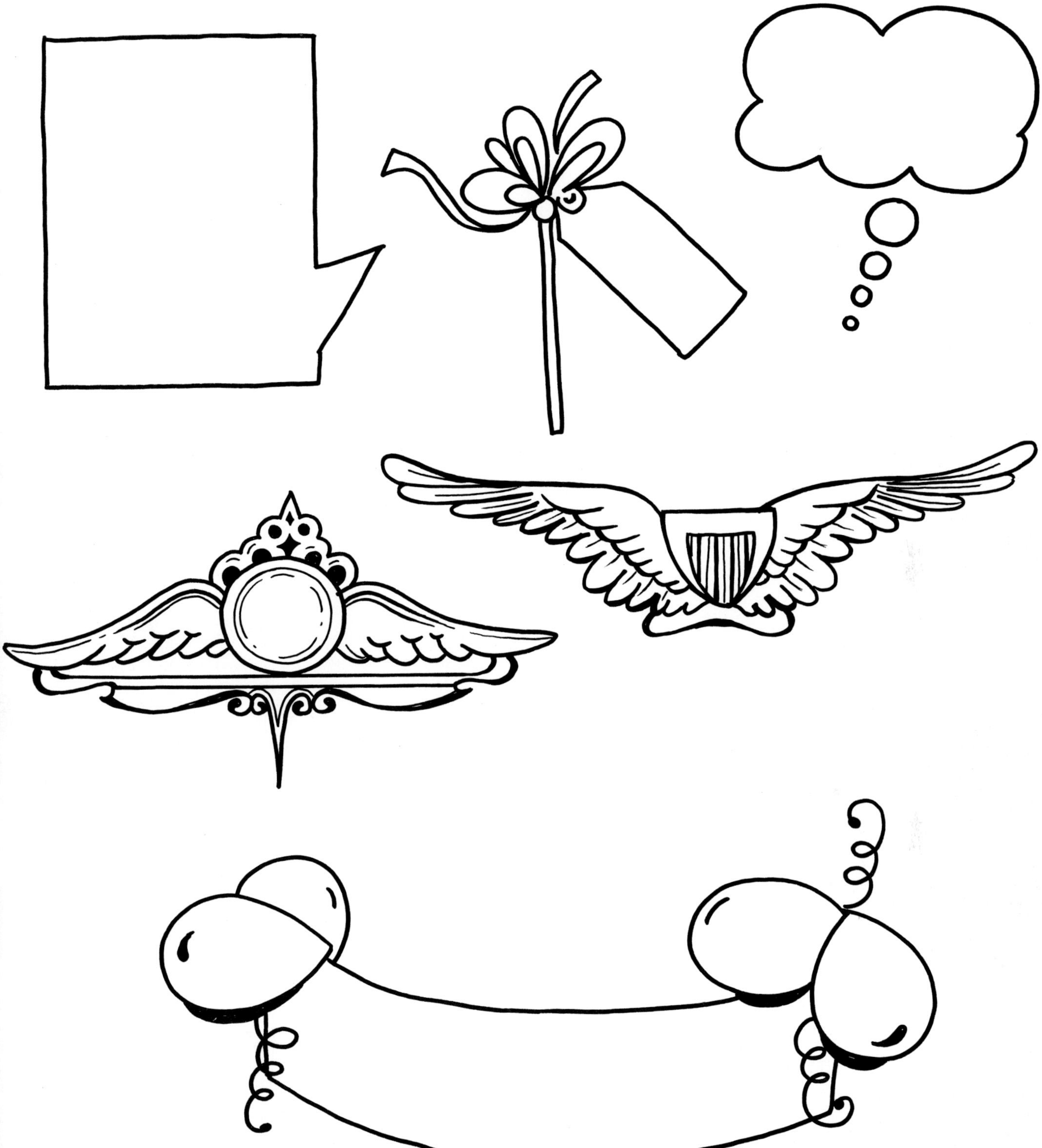

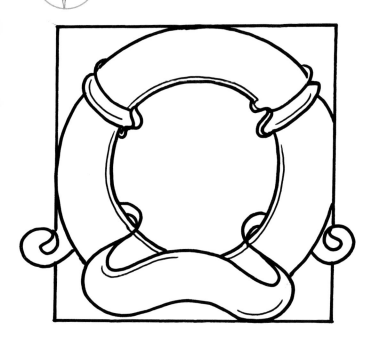

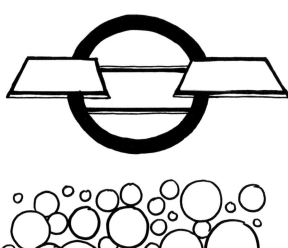

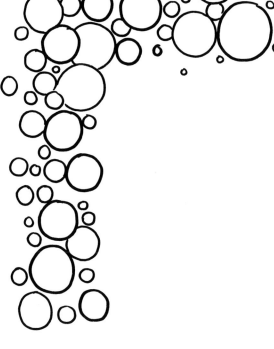

About the author

Sharon Bennett studied graphics and illustration at college before embarking upon a successful career as a packaging designer for various consultancies, eventually becoming Senior Designer for a major confectionary company. In 1986 she started working on a freelance basis in order to divide her time between work and bringing up her family. It was during this time that she moved into the craft world and began to contribute projects to national UK magazines such as *Crafts Beautiful,* and worked on their craft booklets. Sharon has produced five other books for David & Charles, *The Crafter's Design Library: Christmas, The Crafter's Design Library: Florals, The Crafter's Design Library: Celebrations, The Crafter's Design Library: Animals* and *The Crafter's Design Library: Fairies.* Sharon lives with her family in Suffolk, UK.